DRAWING THE HOLOCAUST

A Teenager's Memory of Terezín, Birkenau, and Mauthausen

DRAWING THE HOLOCAUST

A Teenager's Memory of Terezín, Birkenau, and Mauthausen

Michael Kraus

TRANSLATED BY PAUL WILSON

HEBREW UNION COLLEGE PRESS
UNIVERSITY OF PITTSBURGH PRESS

The Paul Wilson translation and select images were previously published in the Czech Republic by Kvartus Media (2013) as *Diary: 1942–45, Notes of the fifteen year old Míša Kraus who survived the Holocaust.*
SNP 3986/1 767 01 Kroměříž CZ

Published by the Hebrew Union College Press, Cincinnati, OH, 45220
and the University of Pittsburgh Press, Pittsburgh, PA, 15260
First paperback edition © 2017, Hebrew Union College Press
Manufactured in the United States of America
Printed on acid-free paper
10 9 8 7 6 5 4 3 2 1

ISBN 13: 978-0-8229-6496-4
ISBN 10: 0-8229-6496-1

Cataloging-in-Publication data is on file with the Library of Congress.

Book design by Paul Neff

CONTENTS

PUBLISHER'S PREFACE vii
AUTHOR'S INTRODUCTION xi
EDITOR'S NOTE xiii
PREFACE 2

I. GHETTO TEREZÍN, 1942–1943

Transport 5
The Home in Hannover Barracks 6
Danger! 9
The Great Roll Call 11
Departure 11
The Journey 13

II. BIRKENAU 1943–1945

GRAVEYARD OF THE VICTIMS OF NAZISM 15
FAMILY CAMP B.II.B, DECEMBER 1943–JULY 1944 15

Arrival 15
Showers 19
Daycare 23
March 7th 24
Arrival! 27
Time Limit Ends, Danger Increases 31
We Take Leave—The Liquidation of B.II.b 31

LIFE WITHOUT PARENTS 35

Men's Camp B.II.d 35
The Front Draws Closer 39
Difficult Wandering 40

III. MAUTHAUSEN

The Second Camp	45
Melk	53
Back to Mauthausen	64
Third Camp	66
Tent Camp	72
Gunskirchen	75
The Big Day—May 7th, 1945—Liberation	78

IV. POST-WAR HARDSHIPS

UNDER THE CARE OF THE US ARMY	81
Hörsching	81
JOURNEY HOME	91
Camp in Linz	95
By Steamboat on the Danube	99
ON RED ARMY TERRITORY	101
Transfer in Melk	101
Journey by Train	104
Wiener Neustadt	105
On Foot to Our Homeland	109
HOME AGAIN	110
Bratislava	110
Prague	113
The Convalescent Home	114
PHOTOS	116
Family Before the War	116
The Terezín Newspaper "Kamarád"	118
The Other Deported Children	120
Transition to "Normal" Life	122
NOTES	124

PUBLISHER'S PREFACE

The Hebrew Union College Press publishes scholarly works as books and as articles in its journals in the fields of Jewish Studies, broadly defined. Since its founding in 1924, the Press has been committed to making available Jewish literature and primary historical sources, often accompanied by translations. The present volume, an illustrated memoir by a fifteen-year-old written shortly after Allied forces brought the dark chapter of Nazi concentration camps to a close, constitutes an unusual primary historical document. The fact that the text was written so close to Michael Kraus's liberation is noteworthy; more remarkable is that he chose to depict memories graphically.

We reproduce in this edition all of the pages with graphic images as unedited facsimiles in order to present the memoir as a historical artifact. The memoir was created like many today—Kraus acquired a series of blank books, one of which was already labeled *Deník*, or "diary," and subsequently filled them with memories in both word and image. The images relate to experiences narrated in the text but also add dimensions to the memoir by evoking what is implicit in the words. The facsimile pages are placed in sequence as close as possible to the texts they illustrate, including pages that indicate volume numbers (IIa, IIb, IIc) and Kraus's section headings.

Those who survived internment in the various kinds of Nazi camps would be in their eighties as this book reaches press. It is possible that additional memoirs will emerge in the future, left behind by survivors who did not wish to speak out directly during their own lifetimes. Our understanding of the Holocaust, despite what is already extensive documentation, will continue to be revised and enhanced with each new document that comes to light.

The Hebrew Union College Press is grateful to the CHARLES AND M. R. SHAPIRO FOUNDATION OF CHICAGO for its generous support of this project. The Center for Holocaust and Humanity Education of Cincinnati, Ohio, directed by Sarah Weiss, is making available, at no cost, materials for educators who may wish to engage *Drawing the Holocaust* in secondary educational contexts. Links to those materials can be found at **press.huc.edu** and **holocaustandhumanity.org**.

David H. Aaron
Jason Kalman

Directors, Hebrew Union College Press
Cincinnati, Ohio

AUTHOR'S INTRODUCTION

It is not easy to write an introduction to the diary I wrote sixty-six years ago, which already had an introduction that was written at the time. The main reason why I set down my experiences from the time of the Nazi occupation was very simple: so that they would not be forgotten. I realized at the time, and I was right, that one can easily forget details and so I thought that it was important to preserve in writing at least an outline of the most important events I had personally lived through. I wanted to preserve them for my descendants without really being fully aware that I would one day establish a family of my own, with children and even grandchildren. Today, all that is a reality; I have a remarkable wife, two wonderful daughters, and four marvelous grandchildren. Had I really intended to pass on the burden of those memories to those seven people? And was my intention a just one? Would the grandchildren be mature enough to understand the events of the last century without suffering nightmares? I have no answers to these questions, but it seems to me that my daughters went through a lot just by growing up in the shadow of a father who bore the mental scars of his devastating experiences in the concentration camps.

At the time, I had no intention of ever publishing my purely personal experiences from the Second World War. I have believed for many years now, however, that it is the responsibility of those few people who survived the concentration camps to pass on their experiences to the greatest number of people. The survivors thought that public awareness of the consequences of a pernicious racism would prevent further genocides from occurring. It turned out that we were quite wrong. Persecution of minorities and genocides have happened repeatedly, and they continue to this day.

With the passage of time, I came to realize that my decision to write down my memories was both proper and important. Writing the diary helped me to overcome the painful and gradual transition to a so-called "normal" life without parents. And it is quite clear to me today that if I had not written down my memories immediately after the war, I would probably never have managed to do so later. When I now read some of these pages again, they seem to be about someone else, because I have forgotten that it was about me. I have kept a diary all my life and, in fact, I have never stopped doing so. In the beginning, it was the only way I had to unburden myself of my own worries and grief. When I got married, I carried on writing out of habit.

I would like mention the people who helped me overcome the loss of my parents and re-enter normal life. They supported me spiritually in my efforts to overcome my great pain and come to terms with the fact that the conditions of life before the war would never return, and that all my relatives, friends, and acquaintances would never arise from the dead. The people who helped me most to make the transition to post-war life were:

Věra Löwenbachová, later Feldmanová (b. August 25, 1910; d. March 23, 2001), looked after me right at the beginning when she discovered that I had survived and was in the rehabilitation center in Štiřín. From there I moved directly to her home in Česká Skalice. Věra was with my mother in the concentration camps, in Stutthof and Praust near Gdańsk, and she had apparently promised my mother that if she survived, she would look after me. Věra became my closest confidant and, until her death, stood in for my mother.

Rudolf Beck (b. December 6, 1900; d. October 16, 1988) and his wife Vilma Becková (b. February 7, 1908; d. December 20, 1982) looked after me in Náchod during my studies at the Jirásek gymnasium from 1945 through 1948, and helped me emigrate to Canada in July 1948, a few months after the communist takeover. During the communist regime, my wife and I visited the Becks six times in all, beginning with our honeymoon in 1963 and, later, with our daughters as well. In 1977, the Becks were able to visit us in the United States. Unfortunately, they did not live to see the Velvet Revolution.

Věra, Rudolf, and Vilma also went through the concentration camps and lost their children to the gas chambers in Birkenau. That was why we understood each other so well. All my life, I have taken strength from the words that Rudolf inscribed for me at Christmas 1946 in a book on the Mauthausen concentration camp: "When cares weigh you down, leaf through this little book and realize how petty it all is compared to what you went through when you were young."

It's important to add that without the help and constant urging of Alena Čtvrečková my recollections would never have made it into print. To that end, she has patiently worked on these pages since 2003.

I believe that my diary will find readers mainly among young people and help them to understand events that, from the perspective of the current day, might seem almost unreal.

Michael Kraus, Brookline, August 2011

EDITOR'S NOTE

The author, as he says himself, began to write a diary while he was still living at home in Náchod, and he continued making entries in the Terezín ghetto. On arrival at the concentration camp at Auschwitz-Birkenau, all his personal effects were confiscated, and all his notes were destroyed.

After his liberation and partial convalescence while still in hospital, he began to draw and make notes again about what he had gone through. This is how Diary I came into being. After his return to Náchod, he continued with Diary II, which filled three small notebooks labeled a, b, and c. He was fifteen at the time and had begun to study at the Náchod gymnasium. He had lost both parents and most of his close relatives, and he found refuge in a family of survivors, Rudolf and Vilma Beck, and later, with an uncle, Hanuš Goldschmid. Between 1945 and 1947, alone and filled with memories of his dear parents, he gradually wrote about his experiences in Terezín, in Auschwitz, and on the first death march in Poland and the second in Austria, out of Mauthausen and its satellite camps in Melk and Gunskirchen. In July 1948, when he left for Canada with the help of the American Jewish Joint Distribution Committee, he took his journals with him. They remained in his private possession.

It was only in 2004 that he sent a black-and-white copy of his notebooks to Náchod. To ensure that the originals would remain undamaged, the author decided to donate them to the United States Holocaust Memorial Museum in Washington, DC. In 2006, he gave color copies of the notebooks to the Jewish Museum in Prague, the Regional Museum in Náchod, and two Israeli memorial institutions: Yad Vashem and Beit Terezín. That was when some of the pages were introduced to the public. In 2006, for instance, they were part of an exhibition devoted to the children from Náchod who were victims of the Holocaust.

From the beginning, it was clear to the small circle of those who had read the notebooks that they deserved to be published. Wherein did their uniqueness lie? In them, the author had accomplished what others of the same age had only attempted to do: to make a record, immediately after his return, of what he considered the most important events and experiences from the concentration camps where he had been confined as a child. At the time, he was filled with hatred toward those who had murdered his parents. As time went by, his memory erased certain details but, even so, the notebooks contain a great deal of them. Because of his studies, and then the preparations to leave the country, the author felt that his time to write was limited, and therefore he reduced his remarks on his stay in the Terezín ghetto to a minimum, to leave more time to record his far more shocking observations from the Nazi concentration camps in Poland and Austria.

A reader unfamiliar with the problems faced by the writer might wonder how a boy who was just entering adolescence could possibly have survived in those circumstances. He was among eighty-nine boys of roughly thirteen to sixteen years old in Auschwitz-Birkenau who, during the liquidation of the so-called family camp B.II.b, were chosen at the last minute to work as servants and messengers. Only a few of them survived to the end of the war in various concentration camps. Later, they began referring to themselves as "The Birkenau Boys." Michael Kraus was lucky; he survived and felt the need to set down his authentic experiences for the benefit of future generations on behalf of the many who did not have that kind of luck.

A boy who is just growing up has no way of filtering his experiences the way adults can, not even with the greater distance of time or under the influence of other pressures and circumstances. His view is subjective, with the directness and sincerity of a child, but tempered by his attempt to be objectively critical.

The editor's aim has been to preserve the language of the notebooks as authentically as possible. After many discussions with friends and experts, any interventions in the text were purely functional, both from the point of view of spelling and comprehensibility. Therefore, the language of the diary remains, as the original does, somewhat bookish in terms of its vocabulary, style, and sentence structure. At the same time, we see how later the text often shifts toward a more conversational style. Because the text makes use of a range of specific expressions used by the prisoners in the Nazi concentration camps, it is worthwhile for readers to take the time to familiarize themselves with such expressions before starting to read. These are printed in italics. The editor has completed the text with notes and explanations.

The author of the diary has been able to provide valuable snapshots of his parents, friends, and the boys who survived the war along with him. Although they now live in different countries, they remain friends and still stay in touch.

Both the author and the editor extend their sincere thanks to Judy Cohen of the Holocaust Museum in Washington, DC, for providing them with high-quality scans of the original notebooks, as well as to the author's fellow survivors and their family members for sending photographs. We also thank Jan Talafant of Kvartus Media publishing house and his collaborators who so generously undertook the production of this book out of friendship to the author. Finally, we thank the Regional Museum in Náchod and the district office in Hradec Králové for their support.

We present this valuable, authentic testimony to the public mainly to help in the task of preserving our memories and carrying on our vigilance regarding all expressions of racial and national superiority, intolerance, and hatred.

Alena Čtvrečková, Náchod, 2011

IIa

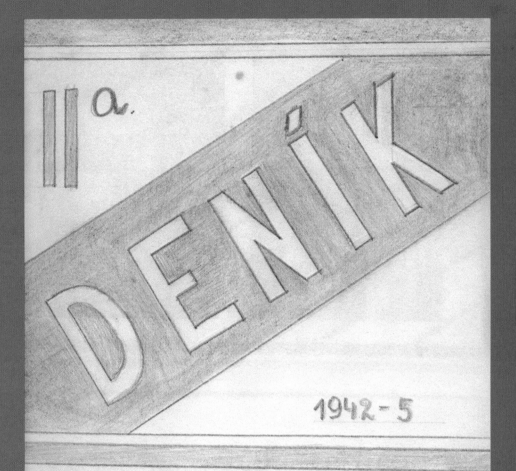

II a.

DENÍK

1942 - 5

Michal Kraus

PREFACE

It has been three years now since I began to write my first diary. At that time, my parents and I were already getting ready to go to Terezín, so there was no shortage of new and interesting things to write about. I spent a lot of time on that diary, as well as on various articles and poems of my own composition. In Terezín such activities increased because I lived in a children's barracks that put out a weekly magazine to which I also contributed.

In December 1943 I was deported to Auschwitz, where all was lost. My beloved books and copybooks were confiscated and burned. No mementos remain from those bad times. Therefore, I want to begin again and briefly recall what I experienced during those six years of German occupation.

It is impossible to describe the horrors of the concentration camps, because no one can feel, from mere words, the real hardships and horrors as they actually occurred. Surely no one could believe the SS methods if he did not experience them on his own skin.[1] Who could feel with us? Who could understand us?

And believe me, although the physical hardships were unbearable and many succumbed to them, the mental hardships were even worse than the physical ones. When I think of it today, I do not want to believe it. I do not want to remember the horrors when I lost my mother and my father, and was expecting death myself, which I escaped only by a miracle.

Those who remained in Náchod did not experience the suffering and disappointment during the seven-year occupation, as did the ten or twelve of us who survived the hell of Nazi brutality and then returned home. We were alive, yes. But it was impossible to call us healthy, because many of us brought severe illnesses home with us.

During the years of persecution, I saw and heard a lot. It was important to me to record it briefly because, as time went on, I found myself forgetting more and more things. When I started to write the first part, I still recalled many details. Two years later, however, I found that I remembered much less of what I wanted to write about, even though each day would have provided a good writer with a wealth of material.

Nonetheless, I want to preserve everything I experienced under the rule of National Socialism, so that my descendants will not forget to despise the Nazi hordes. I use the term "hordes" because there is no other way, in the twentieth century, to describe members of a highly cultured and civilized people that conducted its affairs the way medieval people did some seven hundred years ago.

I therefore can only write about what remains in my memory, the most important events of my life during the war. As I end this introduction, I would like to remember all those who did not survive the Nazi concentration camps. There were many, so terribly many. They suffered horribly. They died in indescribable conditions. And these victims must not disappear from our memory. They must remain exclamation points: Beware of Nazism, fascism and all other forms of lawlessness!

I call these writings a "Diary" but anyone who reads them will realize that the title "Diary" is inappropriate. But these are my experiences, written after the fact, and therefore I will leave the term "Diary" even though it is not entirely correct. I do not intend to write things down in any great detail. I only want to describe the worst days under the rule of Hitler.

Written in the year 1945

I

GHETTO TEREZÍN, 1942–1943

I spent a year in the Terezín ghetto, but as bad as it was, it cannot be compared to a single month in Auschwitz or Mauthausen. Rather than taking time to describe Terezín, I will only briefly record the most important events, because I am writing this during a period in my life when time matters and I would rather describe in greater detail my experiences in the concentration camps.

TRANSPORT

It is Friday November 29, 1942. Outside it's raining, the wind is howling in the crowns of the big oak trees, the thunder is rolling, and lightning is flickering in the dark sky. I am sick, and lying in my bed, overwhelmed by boredom. Suddenly the doorbell rings with a piercing sound. Mother answers the door, and a while later I hear frightened voices in the hall: "Are you sure?" "Yes, yes, I'm quite sure. On the second, those from Pardubice go, on the fourteenth, it will be us!" Upset, I rush out of the room, and soon learn that on the fourteenth of December, we will be leaving for Terezín. Mother is upset but father tries to calm her down: "Our turn had to come sometime. Let us be thankful we were not among the first to go!"

Since then things have been very busy around here. We pack and prepare everything for departure. On the morning of December 14th, about 250 of us report with our luggage to the Náchod railway station. After they take attendance, we climb aboard the train which soon begins to roll. Several dozen people from Náchod are there to say goodbye to us. "When will I see you again?" I think, wiping the tears from my eyes.

The first stop is Hradec Králové, where gold, silver, valuable objects, and money are taken from us. Everyone is given a number he has to wear around his neck. My number is Ch-320.

Two days later we leave Hradec Králové and go directly to Terezín via Prague. The welcome was far from pleasant, and they did not handle us with kid gloves. After an hour's march from the Bohušovice railway station, the gates of the ghetto closed behind us. At first, we were housed in dark barracks called *Schleuse* (H-IV), through which all new arrivals had to pass. There we were registered again, and after three days we were placed in more permanent quarters. Mother and I were sent to L-425, (in block G IV a block designated a formation of buildings arranged in a rectangle), father to the Sudeten barracks (E I).[2] Some weeks later, mother was sent to work in the disinfection laundry and father, as a physician, went to the Dresden barracks.

THE HOME IN HANNOVER BARRACKS

One day a friend came to me and suggested that we move to the children's home in the Hannover barracks (B IV). I agreed, and immediately informed my parents. A few days later they arranged my move. Thus, since March I lived in a home (*Heim*), though it was not well furnished, since it had only just been set up. Some of the time, we studied, only in secret, of course; sometimes we played sports on the large earthworks, called bastions. At least it was more fun than staying in a room doing nothing except waiting for mother to get back from work. At least I was somewhat occupied, and was not thinking all the time about all the hardships that I do not even want to mention. I slept on the top level of a three-tiered bunk. The dusty beams were hung with large cobwebs, and it was impossible to sit up without getting my head tangled up in them.

Vyběhnu rozčílen z pokoje a po kratší debatě se dovídám, že 14ho odjíždíme do Terezína. Matka je rozčílená, ale otec ji chlácholí: „Vždyť jednou musíme příjít na řadu, buďme rádi, že jsme nejeli mezi prvními!"

Od toho dne je u nás ruch. Balíme a připravujeme vše k odjezdu.
Čtrnáctého ráno nastupujeme se zavazadly na náchodském nádraží, asi 250 osob. Po zjištění presentce nastupujeme, a vlak se pomalu rozjíždí.
Desítky Náchoďáků
se s námi loučí. „Kdy
vás zas uvidím," mys-
lím si, stíraje slzy z
očí.

— 12 —

Puní zastávka je v Hradci Králové, kde
je nám odebráno zlato, stříbro, cenné
předměty a peníze. Každý obdrží číslo, které si musí pověsit kolem krku. Moje číslo
bylo „CH 320ʺ.
Po dvou dnech jsme opustili Hradec Králové,
přímo přes Prahu do Terezína.
Uvítání nebylo nijak příjemné a zacházení
nebylo v rukavičkách, ale po hodinovém
pochodu k Bohušovického nádraží se

At the beginning of May 1943, a curfew (*Blocksperre*) was imposed as punishment for those who tried to escape. No one but workers were allowed to leave the building where they lived. I did not see my parents for a long time. But there is an end to everything, and the curfew was lifted at the end of June.

In September, our entire home moved to a building labeled Q 609, which we had spent a whole month fixing up because it was in terrible shape. Our new conditions were somewhat better, because we had real rooms, not an attic. There were twenty-one boys and a youth leader, in a room 6 x 5 meters.[3] We published a magazine called "Kamarád" and there was an atmosphere of good friendship among us.[4]

DANGER!

In January 1943, there was a transport to Poland that we fortunately managed to evade. At the time, five trains departed from Terezín for Birkenau, Riga, Izbica etc., each with 2,000 people on board: men, women, and children, including old people. Of those taken in those transports, fewer than three percent survived.[5]

But in September this terrible danger threatened us again, putting the entire population of the ghetto on edge: transports to Poland! The German command issued an order for 5,000 Jews to get ready to leave within five days. Of course, everyone concerned wanted to avoid deportation, and in the days and nights that followed, there was a deluge of attempts to get taken off the list. But it was all in vain. On the morning of September 6th, 1943, 5,000 persons with their luggage were crammed into two trains, fifty in each closed cattle car. During this fateful period we trembled day and night, wondering when our turn would come. The danger became more imminent when it was rumored that 150 doctors were to be included in the transport, because my father was a doctor. Though no one knew what danger lay ahead, the fear was awful. And the fear turned out to be justified, though no one knew it at the time. We were very, very fortunate. Of those 5,000, a mere ten are alive today.

Zadní vchod
do
Gheta

hou dobu. Ale všechno má svůj konec a i ta „blacksperre" se koncem čer-
vna skončila.
V září se celý náš domov stěhoval do
domu Q 609, který jsme před tím mě-
síc upravovali, neboť byl v nemožném
stavu. Tam byly poměry poněkud
lepší, neboť to byly opravdu pokoje
a ne půdy. V pokoji 6·5 m bylo nás
tenkrát 21 hochů s jedním opatrovni-
kem. Vydávali jsme časopis a mezi námi byl dobrý poměr a kamarád-
ství.

- 17 -

THE GREAT ROLL CALL

Escapes from Terezín were constantly being reported, but the German command did not keep exact records of prisoners, and so it was not easy for them to determine who and how many people were missing. Therefore, one November morning we were awakened at 3:30 and marched from the ghetto to the Bohušovice valley. Police constables and the SS surrounded us. It was a cold day and everyone except the seriously ill had to take part. At about 10 o'clock the camp commander (*Lagerkommandant*) arrived with his staff, and the counting began.[6] But they couldn't get it right and the whole business lasted into the night. It was only after a downpour began that the order was given to march back to the ghetto. A terrible panic broke out, and it was impossible to keep any sort of discipline or order. Warning shots were fired into the air but did not make any difference; everyone just wanted to be the first to get back home. The sounds of children crying, of old people groaning, and the shouts of the leaders—all of that drowned out the shooting. I got home after midnight and collapsed on my bunk, exhausted.

DEPARTURE

Even so, we were caught in the net!

One afternoon, when a cold December wind raged through the snow-covered streets, I went to see my mother in the disinfection laundry. As I entered, I saw her excitedly discussing something with the others: "There's going to be another transport! How awful!" I was immediately reminded of what had happened during the previous transports. I was not certain, yet something told me that we'd be leaving on this transport.

I set about at once to inform myself as thoroughly as I could. The transport was to be announced on the thirteenth, and by noon on the fourteenth everyone who received a notification was to report to designated barracks, that were to be quickly emptied. Anxiety and fear reigned, and everybody trembled when summonses were distributed at night. Oddly enough, I was relatively calm, but something kept telling me that we would be among those unfortunate five thousand. I should have been even more worried but . . . I do not know why I was not. I cannot describe it. All day long, before the notices were to be handed out, my mother hurried from office to office trying to find out whether or not we were to be included in the transport, because if we were, something had be done to prevent it. Once the summonses were delivered, it would be too late.

But despite my mother's efforts, she was unable to learn anything. Nobody wanted to reveal any information, since the punishments for doing so were very severe. There was nothing to be done. On the morning of December 13th, 1943, there was a strange commotion throughout the ghetto. A plague raged in the houses and through the barracks—the transport notices were being distributed. My premonition was right. Our home, Q-609, received fifteen summonses, and one of them bore my name. I expected it.

I started to pack at once. Friends helped me. In the end, I managed to include my most precious things: articles I had written, drawings, and other things. My best friend, Ivan Polák, quickly assembled all the articles from our magazine, *Kamarád*. Then I rushed to my mother and helped her pack foodstuffs. I said goodbye to my friends with a heavy heart; they accompanied me to the assembly point (*Sammelstelle*) where the verification of the lists, the registration, and other matters took place.

Early the next morning, we walked to the train. Long lines of men, women, children, and old people dragged their luggage to the loading ramp. (By this time, a track had been built from Bohušovice to Terezín.) There was the difficult parting from relatives, friends, and mates in front of the *Sudeten* barracks, and then we walked toward the *Jäger* barracks (A-II). On one side the cattle cars stood ready, on the other side, large piles of luggage, and in front of us, a table for registration, along with several SS men, the head of the Czech constabulary, Janeček, and camp commander Burger.[7] It was a colorful collection of German murderers. One by one, we passed between them. Each of us was given a number and with that, we said goodbye to Terezín.

Members of the aid service (*Hilfsdienst*) helped us climb into the high, dark, windowless cattle cars. In the corner stood a pail and a jerry can of water. That is all they gave us for a two-day journey. When fifty of us had gotten on board, they slammed the door shut, sealed it, and we were enveloped in darkness.

THE JOURNEY

Immediately after the door closed, a terrible panic overcame us. Most of the "passengers" in our carriage were old men and women; there were several children, and only few men who might have brought about some order. One of them lit a candle and asked for quiet, which didn't happen right away. Then he began to organize seating arrangements (*Sitzplätze*) and the storing of luggage. With the help of other volunteers, most of the luggage was piled up to the ceiling on one side of the car. Other suitcases were lined along the walls and we sat down on them. About an hour later, we started to move. We felt the train shunting back and forth in the Bohušovice railway station, and then we set off in the direction of Prague.

Right away, in the first hour, a tragic comedy started up. "You are sitting on my bag and it has eggs in it. Get off!" "Where is my bread?" "Damn, my corns!" "The pail is overflowing into my shoes, phooey! I won't let anyone on the toilet! Take it away at once! I'll call the police! Phooey, the stench and all that wetness help, help!" We all realized at once that the lady who was speaking had lost her senses, but we could do nothing to help her.

This went on for two days and two nights, without respite. Sleep was out of the question. Where were we going? Nobody knew. From Prague, the train seemed to be heading northeast, that was all we knew. There was the constant creaking of the carriage wheels as the endless minutes dragged on and on and we listened to the same arguments, without water, without light, and no end in sight.

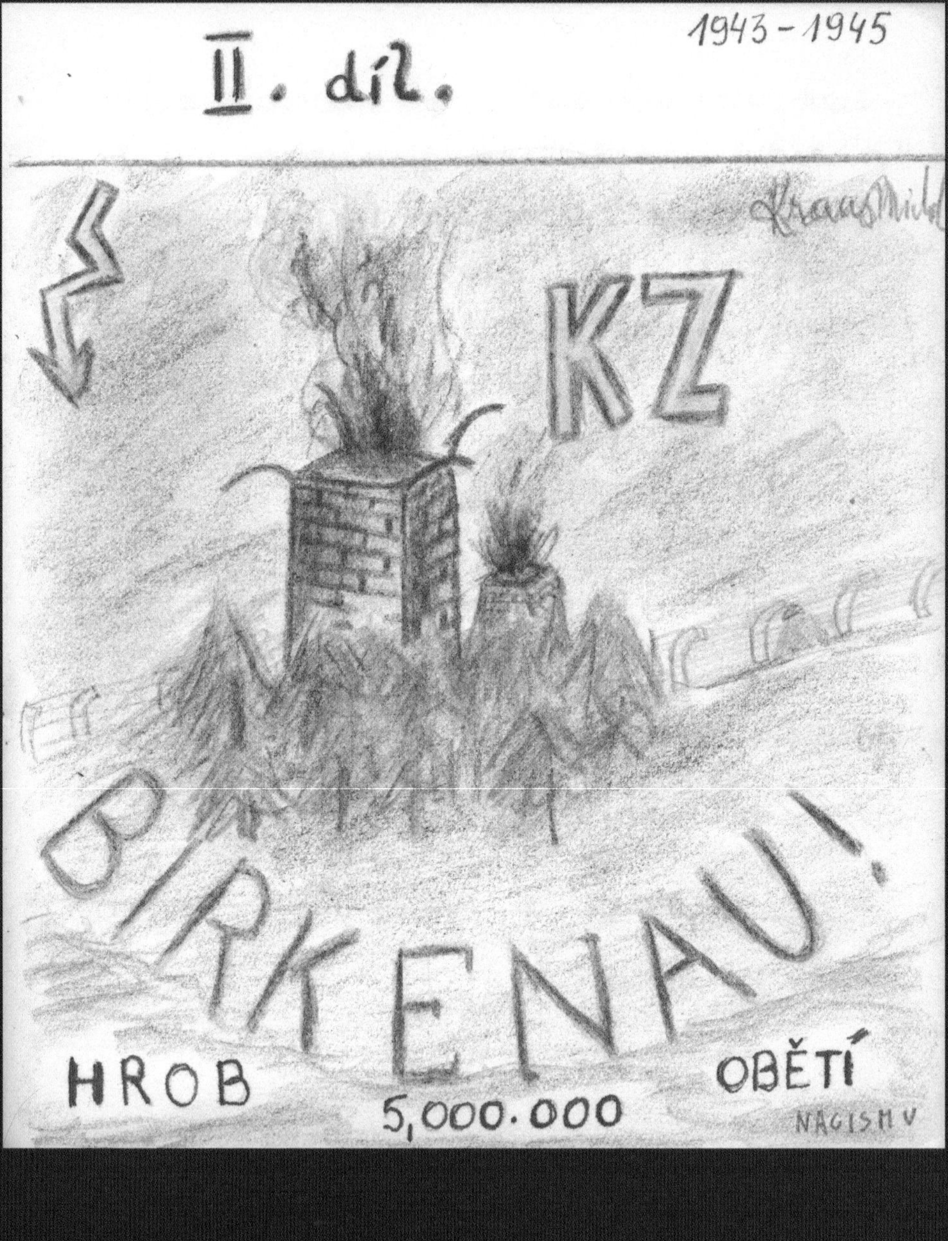
II. díl.
1943 - 1945
KZ
BIRKENAU!
HROB
5,000.000
OBĚTÍ

II

BIRKENAU,
1943–1945

Graveyard of the Victims of Nazism

The second stage of my experience under German rule was Birkenau (Auschwitz II).[8] It is interesting that conditions continued to escalate, in that they became worse and worse. Those first six months in B.II.b were not only difficult physically, they were also a terrible burden emotionally.[9] In fact, it was almost too much for us to bear.

Family Camp B.II.b, December 1943–July 1944

ARRIVAL

Finally, on December 17th, 1943, at half-past eleven at night, the train slowed down and gradually came to a halt. Sharp rays of light entered through a narrow crack in the door. I looked out and was horrified by what I saw through this small, narrow crevice. It was enough to make me turn pale and feel a chill running up and down my spine. I saw so little and yet so much: barbed wire, prisoners in striped uniforms, SS with truncheons. It could only be a concentration camp. But before I could properly absorb this, the door slid open with a great clatter, a sharp spotlight cut thought the darkness, a shot rang out, and several voices yelled in German, "Alles raus, Laufschritt, los, los, raus. Gepäck liegen lassen, raus, raus!" ("All out, run, out, out! Leave the luggage, out! Out!")

I grabbed my knapsack and stepped outside. Next to the wagon stood a soldier, who greeted anyone carrying anything with blows to their backs. SS guards and men in striped uniforms surrounded us and beyond them, there was only barbed wire and more barbed wire. To the left, flames were shooting up from four large, square chimneys. The sky was red; a strange smell hung in the air. A peculiar atmosphere, charged with a kind of tension, a heavy tension.

They herded us onto trucks, and we drove for about ten minutes. I was very upset and looked around for my parents. They might have been just behind me, but I had no idea where they were. As we climbed out of the trucks, an SS guard separated us (the men to one side, the women to the other). Then they took us into a wooden barrack where I found my father. We climbed onto bunks that had neither a straw mattress nor blankets. Now I had a moment to look around. We were in a wooden building about forty meters long and eight meters wide. There were about five hundred of us. On each side of the barrack there were three tiers of bunks. In the middle was a horizontal chimney on which SS guards and prisoners with red armbands strutted. (As we learned later, they were the leaders of the barracks, responsible for order and discipline [*Blockältester*].)

Then a non-commissioned officer (*Unterscharführer*) entered. Everybody stood at attention while he positioned himself in the center of the horizontal chimney and began to talk. Figuratively speaking, it was a "welcome speech" for the new concentration camp victims. His very first words made us sick. He was a strong, tall, thickset man, who gave his rank as SS in charge of roll call (*Rapportführer*) and his name was Buntrock.[10] The prisoners nicknamed him "Bulldog" because of the expression on his face. He gave us a long lecture on how to behave, because we found ourselves in the dreaded concentration camp from where so many death notices were sent: Auschwitz! This camp has been concealed behind names like Birkenau, Waldsee, and others, but in

nau, Waldsee a jinými, ale ve skutečnosti
to byl AUSCHWITZ II. největší KZ této vál-
ky, plod německé kultury, vyvrcholení
germánského sadismu ve 20. století a
nástroj ke zničení těch, kteří se nepodrobí
a nepřidají ke NSDAP. Říše elektrických
drátů, muk a smrti. Peklo na zemi.
Zkrátka vylíčil nám vše stručně na
čem jsme, při čemž mu pomáhala jeho
sukovice a několik blokových.
Bylo toho dost, až moc, co jsme se v
té hodince dozvěděli a domyslili to,
co nám sám neřekl. Vždyť to byl
esesák, lotr, sadista a vrah, jako byli
všichni ti páni v Osvěnčíně.

Vyhnali nás z blocku, ustavili do pětice a šlo se. Mrzlo. Starci se smekali na hladké cestě, pokryté sněhem i ledem. Byli odkopnuti surovými blokführery do příkopu, kde za několik hodin skončili svůj těžký život.
Několikráte nás pak počítali před táborem.
Cesta do sauny vedla kolem krematoria III. a IV. Nevěděli jsme však tenkráte, kolem jakých hrůz jdeme. Po dvaceti minutách došli jsme ke rovné, velké budově s vysokými okny. Sauna.
Vešli jsme dveřmi s nápisem: Nejsi „Strana"!

reality it was Auschwitz II, the largest concentration camp in this war, a product of German culture, the peak of Germanic sadism in the Twentieth Century, an instrument for the destruction of those who would not submit to and join the NSDAP (*Nationalsozialistische Deutsche Arbeiterpartei*). It was an empire of electric fences, suffering, and death—a hell on earth. Buntrock briefly described our situation, aided by his truncheon and several heads of work groups (*Kapos*). We learned much during that lesson, too much, in fact, and we were able, in our thoughts, to fill in what he did not tell us himself. After all, he was a member of the SS, a thug, a sadist and a murderer, just like all the masters of Auschwitz.

SHOWERS

The next evening, employees of the registry office (*Schreibstube*) began calling us out by name in alphabetical order. Our turn came around 10 o'clock. There were about 400 whose names began with "K." They escorted us to another barrack, where each of us was given a small piece of paper with a number on it. We then proceeded to the place where they did the tattooing. They tattooed the number 168497 on my left forearm and 168498 on my father's. Then we went to be registered. After all the forms were filled out, we were taken outside where they separated fathers from the boys and the small children. The adults went to the showers (*Sauna*).

The next day it was our turn. They drove us out of the barrack, lined us up in rows of five and marched us on. It was below zero. Old men slipped and fell on the smooth path, which was covered by snow and ice. The brutal block commander (*Blockführer*), a member of the SS, kicked them into the ditch, where their difficult lives ended several hours later. They counted us several times outside the camp.

The route to the showers took us past Crematoria III and IV. At that time we were unaware of what horrors we were going past. Twenty minutes later we arrived at a large, new building with high windows— the showers. We entered by doors marked "Unclean Side." There we undressed in a large hall. Children under fifteen years put their clothes

Tam jsme se svlékli ve velkém sále. Děti do 15 let odevzdaly své šatstvo na věšáky, dospělí je házeli do pytlů.

Pak byla prohlídka, po níž jsme se šli koupat. Asi za 4 hodiny jsme obdrželi své vydesinfikované šatstvo. Dospělí však dostali hrozné hadry a dřevěné

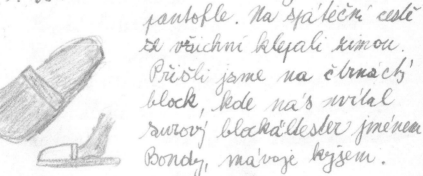

pantofle. Na spáteční cestě že všichni klejali zimou. Přišli jsme na čtrnáctý block, kde nás uvítal surový blockälltester jménem Bondy, ma'voje kyjem.

-39-

Tento vyvrhel a vrah byl opravdu hrozný člověk. Celý den jen lítel po blocku, hulákal, klel a mlátil.

Našili jsme si čísla, na kabát i na kalhoty. Pak nás nacpali po šesti do jednoho patra

ledy 18. na bom! To byl náš nový byl." Každý obdržel jednu slabou deku. K obědu, jako vždy, bylo ¾ litra švínové "olichty". Po obědě byl dlouhý apell. Malé děti plakaly a volaly po malkách. A tak to šlo den za dnem.

- 40 -

jednotvárný, skoro beznadějný život. Otce ani matku jsem dlouho neviděl. Teprve asi za deset dní, jsem přes přísný

HLÍDKOVA BUDKA. (V ZIMĚ).
1. Balony, které obklopují továrnu na munici.

zákaz navštívil otce, který byl na 16. bloku. Byl nemocen. Podvýživa a zima v tak krátkém čase změnily drahého otce. Byl bledý, slabý a velmi hubený. Sháněl jsem pro něho léky a bílý chléb. Nic na plat, byl stále nemocen. V lednu musili muži ven, nosili kameny. Úmrtnost stoupala. Hromady mrtvol se denně kupily za všemi bloky.

- 41 -

- 22 -

on hooks; adults threw their clothes into sacks. Following an inspection, we went under the showers. After about four hours we got our disinfected clothes back. The adults, however, were given only awful rags and wooden clogs.

On the way back, we were all shivering from the cold. We were sent to Block 14 where a brutal, truncheon-wielding barracks elder named Bondy welcomed us. This outcast and murderer was a truly horrible person. All day he ran around the barrack, yelling, cursing and beating people. We had to sew numbers on our jackets and pants. Then they crammed eighteen of us onto each three-level bunk. This was our new "home." Everyone got a thin blanket. For lunch, as always, we were given three quarters of a liter of turnip "slop."

After lunch there was a long roll call. Small children cried and called out for their mothers. This went on day after day. It was a monotonous, almost hopeless life. I saw neither my father nor my mother for a long time. It was only about ten days later that I visited my father in Block 16, though it was strictly forbidden. He was sick; it had not taken long for the undernourishment and the cold to change my dear father. He was pale, weak, and very thin. I scrounged medicines and white bread for him, but it was no help; he remained ill.

In January the men had to work outside, carrying stones. The death rate increased. Heaps of corpses piled up behind all the barracks. We were quarantined for one month. Later I saw my mother; she was in Block 11, and later moved to Block 5. She too had changed a lot during one month.

DAYCARE

Camp B.II.b was the only family camp (*Familienlager*) for Jews in all of Auschwitz.[11] As the name implies, families could be together— but that meant together in one camp, not in a single block. Camp B.II.b already held the so-called "old" transport, people who had arrived from Terezín in September 1943, consisting of men numbered from 146,000 to 148,000 and women from 57,000 to 59,000. Our "new" transport consisted of men numbered from 168,000 to 171,000 and women from 70,000 to 73,000. Among those in the old transport from Terezín was the youth leader Fredy Hirsch, a man who lived only for young people and later gave his life for them. Back in Terezín, amid all that misery, he had managed to acquire all kinds of sports equipment, and he was able to do the same in Birkenau. Fredy first became a camp head in charge of work details (*Lagerkapo*), but later he gave up that high function and reverted to his previous role as youth leader (*Jugendleiter*). He was able to persuade the camp commander to exempt children up to the age of sixteen from standing in long roll calls in the cold, two or three times a day. Children and youths were counted in a specially designated block where Fredy Hirsch had tables and benches built for them. This gave them a great advantage. His actions resulted in saving the lives of many children, though most of them, alas, later perished anyway.

After the January quarantine, members of our "new" December transport were finally allowed to move around the camp a little. The adults were put to work. Children were moved with the others to Block 18, and from there, starting in February, they went each morning to the children's daycare (*Tagesheim*), returning only in the evening. At this time I was in this group because I was thirteen and a half years old. Up to the age of fourteen, children received better soup and a larger ration of jam.

My mother was able to get work in the laundry. She worked either during the evening shift or in the morning. I saw her only rarely. Father remained ill. Later, when he felt better, he was put to work examining clothes for lice, something all the other doctors did as well. It was a very important task, because lice spread typhus.

MARCH 7th

The days dragged on, and every hour brought some new trials—cold and hunger—that was camp life in B.II.b. At the beginning of March, rumors started that the old transport would leave, but nobody knew when or to where. These were so-called *bonkes*, or panic-mongering rumors.

Dostávali jsme do čtrnácti let lepší polévku a větší příděl marmelády.

Matka se tou dobou uchytila v prádelně. Pracovala buď večer neb ráno. Viděl jsem ji jen zřídka. Otec byl stále nemocen.

Později, když mu bylo lépe, prohlížel dětstvo na vši, což dělali všichni lékaři. Bylo to velmi důležité, neboť veš vši byla nebezpečným tvorem, roznášela Syphus.

achtung!
LAUSEGEFAHR !!

Desinfekcion !

Zugang:

Můj tatínek byl tou dobou nemocen,
Když byl vyprázdněn lékařský blok č. 24.
byl přemístěn na krankenbau – blok 28.

Dělali jsme co jsme mohli,
ale jeho zdravotní stav se stále horšil

A jednou v noci to přišlo.
Byli jsme vyrušeni ze spánku halošem aus. Byla blokspere.
Přijel terezínský transport.
Druhého dne jsme vyklouzli z bloku a šli se podívat, nepři-
jel-li někdo známí

– 49 –

PÁSKA BLOCK-
ÄLTESTRA
(Blokového)

BLOCK 3

Even so, on the morning of March 7th, the entire Camp B.II.b was lined up for the roll call.[12] The numbers of the old transport were read, and around noon they all left the camp in groups. There were many sad partings, as many of my relatives left with them. For two days the entire [old] transport was quarantined in Camp B.II.a, and then they were gone. They were taken away during the night. The big question was "where to?" Later we learned that they had all been sent to the gas chambers. Fredy Hirsch went with them, along with the children with whom he had lived and worked and for whom he also died. Only a few physicians and twins were spared annihilation. This was the fate of most transports that came to Birkenau from Poland, Italy, Hungary and the other countries occupied by the Germans.

ARRIVAL!

For some time there had been talk that another transport would be arriving from Terezín. It was frequently rumored that the transport was already on its way, or even that it was already at the arrival (*Zugang*) ramp. There was always some truth in every rumor, and so that pessimistic news, too, turned out to be correct. It was May. The sun was already blazing down on the barren surfaces, the swamps and the muddy paths. Work commandos were constructing a road through the camp (*Lagerstrasse*), and the maintenance team (*Stubendienst*) prepared empty barracks for the announced arrivals.

My father was sick at that time. When the doctors' Block 24 was emptied, he was moved to Block 28, which was called the infirmary (*Krankenbau*). We did what we could, but his health continued to get worse.

And one night it came. We were awakened from our sleep by the rumble of lorries. A curfew was in force. The transport from Terezín had arrived.[13] The next day we slipped out of the barracks to see if somebody we knew had come. There was chaos in the camp; people were beaten. The SS ran around the camp like madmen. The new transport was a special exception. People were not sent to the showers, which was a great advantage for them. Their tattooed numbers started at A-100 and went up from there.

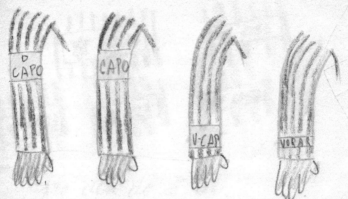

V táboře byl nepořádek. Všude se mluvilo.
Rozzuření esesáci lítali po lágru jako
zběsilí.

Nový transport byl však výjimkou
všech. Nešel do sauny, což bylo ohromné
plus. Tetovaná čísla byla od A-100 výše.
Mezi příchozími bylo mnoho známých,
kamarádů i příbuzných. Byl zřízen
ještě jeden heim na bloku 29

-50-

pro děti do 10. let.

A zase plynuly dny, jeden jako druhý, jaxi každý přinášel novou nepříjemnost. Appely byly dlouhé a nepříjemné pod praxičim sluncem.

Kapitola 8.

»LHŮTA SE KONČÍ, NEBEZPEČÍ STOUPÁ «

- 51 -

SPORT PŘI
APELU

lidských těl.   Můj otec byl stále nemocen.
Ležel na krankenbau 3b. Chodili jsme
k němu denně. Mluvil velmi pesimisticky.
Slábl. Bylo mi strašně.
Pracoval jsem tenkrát on 3 neděle u p.
Kuneveldra ve Wäscherei. Dostával jsem
víc polévky a zulage (salám).
Byly to tenkrát srdečné dny. Něco hrozné-
ho se nad námi stahovalo.

- 53 -

Selekce v táboře

Nevěděl jsem tehdy, že se již nikdy, nikdy
neuvidíme. Ani rozloučit jsme se nemohli.
Snad to bylo lepší. A pak vybroli nás,
98 hochů. Ostatní měli zůstat – a ......
Hrůza pomyslet. To loučení s otcem bylo
strašné, vidím ho před sebou, hubeného,
nemocného, jak plakal – on, vždy dobrý
ke všem lidem a nyní jsem jej

Krematorivm
I.

opustěl, zanechároji
jej smrti. Nemohu na to již myslet, neboť
to byl nejhrovnější okamžik v mém životě.

—

Odvedli nás troše, jak do směrem ke
sauně!— Krematorium se k nám blížilo.
Byli jsme udiveni, když nás zavedli
do sauny v cikánském táboře a
jak na 13 blok v mämulogru.

- 56 -

would never, ever see each other again. We were not even able to say goodbye. Perhaps it was better that way.

Then Mengele selected us, eighty-nine boys in all. The others were to stay—and . . . it is too awful to think about! Taking leave of my father was terrible. I can see him standing in front of me, emaciated, sick and crying, he who had always been so kind to everyone and now I was leaving him to die. I cannot think about it because it was the most dreadful moment of my life.

They marched us to the gate, and then toward the showers. The crematorium drew closer. We were astonished when they took us to the showers in the gypsy camp and then to Block 13 in the men's camp (*Männerlager*).

It is painful to remember all those who stayed behind in B.II.b and were later gassed; hundreds of acquaintances and friends—those who never came back from the transports.

Life without Parents

MEN'S CAMP B.II.d

We came to the block that housed the prisoners who worked in the gas chambers and crematoria (*Sonderkommando*).[16] In the beginning we were not too badly off. A lot of food had been stolen from the Hungarian transports and it ended up mainly in the men's camp. I became a messenger (*Läufer*) for the work unit responsible for items like blankets, dishes, and clothing (*Unterkunft*). I met many people, good ones and bad ones. My life at that time was reasonable, under the circumstances.

On July 11th, I could not sleep. The night was clear and the sky was red. And out there—somewhere out there—no, I cannot talk about it. On July 11th, the Nazis killed my father—tortured him to death. I clenched my fists, I cried, I promised cruel revenge. Many of us lost their dearest ones on that day.

ještě nikdy neviděl.

Devetitisíce(?) denně šli na popravu.

Vyhnali je z rajónu rovnou na smrt. A někdy i rovnou do ohně. A na to jsme se měli my dívat z lágru?

SELEKCE — VZPOURA.

Na prankenlaulagru byly pravidelné selekce těžce nemocných, "müselmanů". Ale jednou, a zejména a já přímo, to přišlo i na nás – mladé.

Museli jsme se svlékovat a kdo byl menší určité délky, byl zapsán. Ale naštěstí do raportführer poručil, že asi 30 žáků zůstalo v lágru – takže jim zachránil životy.

Byli však rozesláni do vážných okolních táborů na práci.

Jednou, asi na podzim byl odeslán velký transport židů z našeho tábora. Odešlo s nimi i mnoho našich kamarádů.

- 60 -

weapons, set fire to Number 3 and tried to escape. Most of them, however, were shot far from the camp.

October Transports

The previous winter, all the gypsies who were interned in B.II.e were gassed. In October 1944, transports started to arrive again from Terezín.[18] In B.II.e they went through selection by Mengele and were sent to other camps, where many perished. There I met Rudolf Beck, Max Haas, Tom Löwenbach and others.[19] They all soon departed.

Executions

We were often forced to witness executions, mainly of Russians, Poles and Jews. Those who belonged to the same nationality of the persons sentenced to die were gathered in a large area near the kitchens to watch. Usually two or three people were hanged at a time. They were being punished for attempting to escape. I vaguely recall that once, six heads of work groups escaped, among them our boss (*Oberkapo*) from the equipment unit.

Air Raids

Russian and American planes flew over us every day, dropping bombs nearby. A bomb fell on the SS camp. Unfortunately it killed two prisoners, but no SS guards.

THE FRONT DRAWS CLOSER

By now, transports were leaving for work camps, but these were regular departures. The chimney had ceased belching out smoke and a thin layer of snow covered Birkenau when, during the night of January 18, 1945, orders came down that an already scheduled transport was to assemble immediately. The order applied to half of the B.II.d camp. It left in the morning. A new order was issued to burn all card catalogues, lists, and other written documents. In the afternoon it was our turn, the other half of B.II.d. The departure went slowly because other camps were being liquidated at the same time.

Finally, at long last, the front line drew near. Only the sick and those who were twins remained. The rest of us were driven into Auschwitz I, where we received food rations and, while it was still night, we started walking, walking all night. It was below zero. Prisoners wearing wooden clogs and poor clothing began collapsing. Those in the rear who could not keep up were shot in the head at close range. It was horrible! The road was lined with corpses from previous transports that had gone ahead of us.

DIFFICULT WANDERING

In January 1945—the final year of the Second World War—I went through the so-called Death March. Yes, it was a death march, because it claimed many victims and only a few of us survived. We walked for three days. The number of dead who had been shot ahead of us kept increasing. The two guards behind us who were shooting prisoners unable to continue walking were kept very busy. The shattered heads of the victims were a horrible sight. (The SS guards held the rifle muzzles directly to their heads.) At night they herded us into some kind of farm. Some of us slept on hay, others in the stable; most froze outside. Due to inadequate clothing, many literally froze to death or were shot because their feet had become frostbitten. I remember one poor fellow—a non-commissioned SS officer ordered him to run from the farm toward the guards and then shot him in the back. The third bullet from his revolver killed him. This is how our "guardians" amused themselves.

All I remember was that this occurred in the district of Pless. They drove us further, on to Loslau, where they crammed an impossible number of us into railway carriages.[20] There wasn't even enough room to sit down. And so, with no food, we traveled for four days in open freight cars toward a new concentration camp. We first assumed that we were going to Gross-Rosen, because transports ahead of us had gone there. But when we arrived in Bohumín, we found that the tracks were cut off so that we had to turn back.

The Poles treated us shamefully. They gave us nothing at all. They did not even react to the heaps of corpses that lined the roads or piled up in towns and villages. My opinion of Poles has not changed to this day. By contrast, our people—the Czechs—behaved decently. In every railway station, despite the great danger, they tossed rolls, bread, gingerbread, and other food into our carriages. The railway employees gave us their mid-morning snacks. Yes, I was back in Bohemia, even though I was only passing through, but my people did not disappoint me.

Many people died on the way. For a long time we did not know where we are being taken. Only when we passed through ruined Vienna did we realize that they were taking us to Mauthausen—that awful place where so many of our people—including some from Náchod—had already perished.[21]

If I remember correctly, I was in a carriage with Walter Spitzer, our record-keeper (*Schreiber*), as well as with Míša Grünwald and three dentists for whom he had been a messenger in Auschwitz.[22] A work group leader occupied an entire corner. A German Jew from the infirmary composed nice songs. On the way we drank water from the locomotive. With a few exceptions, there was nothing to eat.

In such a condition we were roused one morning from our drowsy state (sleep was impossible) on a bridge over the Danube. The sight before our eyes was terrifying. Over those huge, notorious quarries rose the stone fortress of the infamous death camp—Mauthausen. Huddled beneath it, pressed against the rock, was a small town. It was five o'clock in the morning when they drove us out of the wagons. The piles of corpses that remained behind were a horrible sight. They lined us up in rows, and at eight o'clock, led us through the small town full of German signs advertising companies. The icy path up a steep slope was not easy for everybody to climb, and that too claimed its victims.

At the top, work was in full swing. We passed a row of SS barracks and arrived at large stone fortifications that surrounded the main camp. There were high guard towers, machine guns and barbed wire. We came to a gate. They counted us and we entered. Once more, we were inside the barbed wire of a concentration camp. Mauthausen!

II b

DENÍK

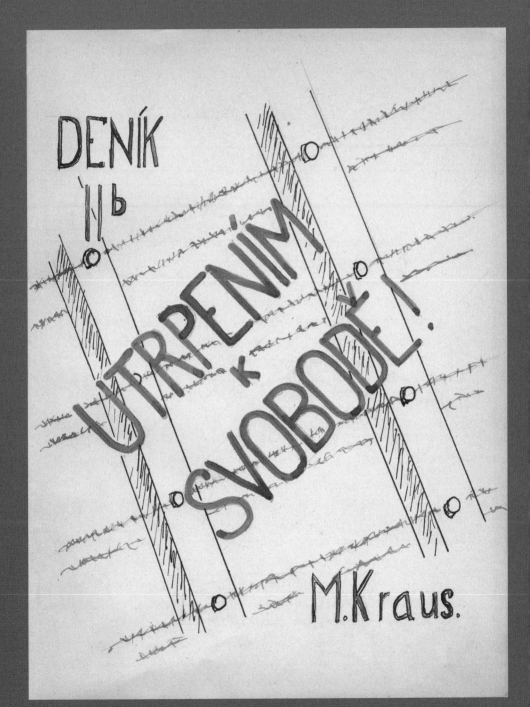

We waited about ten minutes until there were twenty of us, and then we trotted off to a block, I think it was number 21. There, many poor wretches were already assembled. Our personal information was taken down and we each got a metal strip with a number that was fastened to our wrist by a wire. In this way, many prisoners were scratched and seriously harmed when the scratches resulted in blood poisoning. At night, we slept in groups of five on narrow bunks. For dinner we had a disgusting soup that was practically inedible, but we had had nothing to eat for a week, if not longer. I hardly slept at all as I had to be careful not to fall off the bunk.

We were awakened early next morning. The whole day was taken up by formalities such as registration and check-ups. The food was miserable and included a smelly piece of melted butter. The next day we were all sick. The third day in Mauthausen, we were issued clothing. It was impossible, made of coarse cloth.[23] Those of us who had placed articles of clothing into sacks got them back. I didn't find mine until the fourth day, but not everything was there. That day there was also the first roll call. Míša Grünwald and I got bread and a pocketknife (a rarity there) from a Czech; I think his name was Franta (there were many Czechs in Mauthausen).

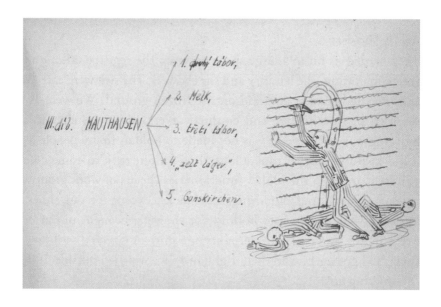

1. DRUHÝ TÁBOR.

I. Zase „Sauna."

nahnali nás na velké prostranství, které bylo mezi Sheebatulou, krematoriem, prádelnou a saunou. Nemocné donesli k barákům, kde je položili na rozryklou zem. Nás seřadili do pětistupu a několikráte počítali. Sauna nebyla velká, nebyla přijemná napro tolik lidí jako osvětinská. Trvalo dlouho, než jsme přišli na řadu. My, děti a také vyšší funkce, (kapové, blockältesti) jsme si dávali věci do vzadu, aeme lot. Tak nás hnali pod teuči sprchy, na pět minut ven, každému holili laď spodky nebo košili. Viděl-to to jeden Čech, tak jsem dostal oleji. a hned ven, na mráz. čekali jsme asi 10 minut než nás bylo oblect a

10

I don't remember how many days we spent there. We were housed in several blocks. One day they lined us all up. They called out all the children and also many adults; almost the entire transport that arrived from Auschwitz. Only some highly placed "shirkers" and the sick remained. Some went to Gusen. They frightened us by saying that we would be sent to do hard labor. The worst was yet to come. They lined us up by fives in front of the registry office. We were a row of five Czech boys.

We Travel Again

They separated us into groups of a hundred and sent us to the gate where they counted us again, while the highest-ranking SS officer of Mauthausen looked us over. At the gate, the guards stood ready and took up positions on both sides of our transport. As far as I can remember, we were marched first between the SS barracks. Then a view opened before us. Beneath us was a football field where military cars and trucks were parked. Beyond them were barracks surrounded by barbed wire. In front of us was a road leading into town; on the left were high stone ramparts with guard towers and machine guns, and here and there were smaller caliber anti-aircraft guns. There were guards and barbed wire everywhere and exhausted prisoners surrounded by SS guards with bullwhips.

Thus we descended into the town. At the railway station we waited a long time for the wagons. I was astonished by the townspeople. They looked at us as though we were wild animals or real criminals who had to be kept under guard. We were crammed into cattle cars. Still, compared to other days of transport, we traveled quite well. I don't know how long we were on the way. There were two guards in each cattle car, nice guys who gave us bread with butter and other "goodies." On the way we saw mostly military trains, shot up carriages, and trains carrying the wounded.

Melk an der Donau is a very nice town. Above the river there is a beautiful monastery (at the time it was a hospital for the SS).[24] We got out at a small station. The guards once again lined us up by fives and soon we set off walking. The former barracks leader from Block 13 at

poklusem na nějaký blok, myslím, že to byla jedna-
dvacítka. Tam již bylo mnoho nebožáků koncentrova-
ných. Sepisovali tam s námi jména národnie a dostali
jsme tam plíšek s číslem, který se k nuce přidělával
na číslem. Takto se již mnoho věcně učinit povolilo
tím, že z oděvu a obuvi dostali svar time.
Přes noc jsme spali po pěti na jednom úzkém kanále.
K večeři byla hnusná polévka, která se skoro nedala
jíst, ale mi neměli v žádech týden, re-li-vše.
Nespali jsme skoro vůbec, neboť jsem musel dávat
pozor, abych nespadl. Brzy ráno nás vzbudilo.
Celý den se dělali formality. Zápisy, prohlídky
atd. Jídlo bylo mizerné. Fasovali jsme též kus
smradlavého vyškvařeného másla. Bylo nám
druhý den špatně. Třetí den v manklansanu
se fasovalo šatstvo. Úplně nemožné – drill.
My, kteří jsme je dávali do pytlů,
dostávali jsme své. Já je nosil
od 4 dne, no však všechno. Jen

den byli první apell. Já a Míša grünbaum*wald* jsme
dotali od nějakého Čecha, Franta se myslím
jmenoval, (Čechů bylo v Mauthausenu hodně)
Mléka a kapesní nůž, což tam bylo vzácností.
Nepamatuji se, kolik dní jsme tam strávili.
Jednoho dne nás sřadili. Byli jsme v několika
blocích. Vyvolali všechny děti a i mnoho dospě-
lích. Skoro celý transport, který přišel z Osvětimi.
Jen vzrou "ulepšáá" a nemocní. Někteří šli do guze-
nu.
Strašili nás všelijak, že jsme na nějakou těžkou
prací. Nebylo to však ješte nejhorší. Před
schreibstubou nás sřadili do peti-
stupů. Udělali jsme pětici českých
chlapců.

II. Znovu cestujeme.

Po stovkách nás oddělili a

které musno hlídat. Nacpali nás do dobytčáku.
Jelo se nám tenkráte docela dobře, proti jiným
pozdějším dnům na cestách. Nevím, jak dlouho
jsme jeli. Ve vagoně byli dva posti, milý chlopi.
Dali nám chleba a máslem a ještě různé
„dobroty". Cestou jsme viděli samé vojenské
vlaky, rozstřílené garnitury a vlaky s raně-
nými.
Melk an der Donau je velmi pěkné město. Má nad
řekou i pěkný zámeček (tenkráte tam byl SS lazaret.) Vystoupili jsme na menším nádraží. Posti
nás sehnali do 5ti skupin a za chvíli se
šlo. Nás dělí, si oral na starosti náš bývalý blockältester ze 13. blocku a několikaletý-
grun. nějaký roksdeutscher.

Melk an der Donau

2. MELK!

I. Brambory!!

Pochodovali jsme dlouho zasněženými městem,
ulicemi, které lemovaly krásné vily se
zahradami. Všude samý nápis – německé
spolky a úřady – samý plakát. Na ulicích
nebylo skoro lidí, pro špatné počasí.
Pak jsme šli do prudkého kopce. Stmívalo
se již, když nás počítali před branou a
pouštěly po stovkách do lágru.

15

the men's camp took charge of us children. He was some sort of an ethnic German (*Volksdeutscher*).

MELK

Potatoes!

We marched for a long time through the snow-covered town, along streets lined with beautiful villas and gardens. There were signs everywhere—for German associations and offices—and many posters. There were hardly any people in the streets because of bad weather. Then we walked up a steep incline. It was already dark when they counted us in front of the gate and let us into the camp in groups of a hundred.

They lined us up in a large open space between the tenement houses. Because the storm swept snow into our eyes, we could scarcely see. They counted us again. The camp commander, who was furious, cursed us. I do not know how long we stood there, but it seemed an eternity to us. Finally they separated the young ones and sent us up to the first floor of the largest stone building, where they assigned us a room. They gave us soup, registered us, examined us for lice, and then we fell asleep. It was like being in paradise. How many weeks had gone by since we had been able to sleep? The last time was in Birkenau, about January 15th. After that terrible journey, the rapid succession of events and the terrible cold, it was amazing.

Emil from Block 13 became the leader. He favored the Poles and simply beat us Jews. He seemed to remember me because I was a messenger in Birkenau. Some of the boys were given good positions. Míša Grünwald was made head of the maintenance team for a block; Harry Lewit went to serve in the registry office and later was assigned to the camp commander; Karol went to the headquarters of the block commanders (*Blockführerstube*), etc. The next day they picked about twenty-five of us, the tallest. I was paired with Harry Osers.[25] They assigned us to several blocks as the maintenance team. I am not sure what the number of the block was to which we were assigned. I think it was 9. We had a good barracks elder and record keeper and all together, it was good. Like most of the blocks, ours was a former garage or perhaps a warehouse of some kind. Harry and I had a lot of work, but it was still a bit better than going with the others to the potato-house. We could have as much soup as we wanted, and sometimes there was leftover bread.

But I was destined not to stay with Harry for long. A certain Zbyšek, who knew the record keeper, was put in my place. The next day I set off to work with the others. But such changes occurred on other blocks as well. Some boys were thrown out because they were too small, others because they did very little work, and so on. I remember that Chaim Grün and Harry Goldberger had to carry out a corpse on the very first day.[26] The mortality rate in the camp was terrible, something I realized only later.

And so I would go to the kitchen early in the morning and return late at night. It was terrible work. The wet, rotting potatoes had to be peeled with sharpened pieces of metal. We could not take potatoes home with us because we were searched daily. We poured the dirty potatoes into large basins. The dampness deprived many of their health. The monotonous work was exhausting. Poor tools crippled our hands. These were awful times. Some boys, mainly Russians, at times managed to smuggle potatoes out, and then either boiled them or traded them for bread. They were often caught and beaten. The master sergeant in the SS (*Hauptscharführer*) who served as the kitchen boss was terrible, a criminal type. I cannot remember how long I worked there. It might have been a month, perhaps longer.

Messengers at the Headquarters of the Block Commanders

The messengers (*Läufer*) at the headquarters of the block commanders (*Blockführerstube*) at the main gate were Karol and a Dutchman, or perhaps he was of another nationality. One morning a work group leader came from the electricians saying that he needs a servant (*Pipl*). Bednárek suggested me. But I did not want to go, and the work group leader left. On the third day the camp head in charge of work details came and said that both runners were sick and he needed a substitute. They called me again and the next morning, while it was still dark, I got up much earlier than the others, and went to the gate. It was certainly not enviable work.

Before I describe the part of my life in Melk when I worked at the gate, I must mention something in general about the camp. At that time I was in a position to observe conditions very closely. I no longer know how many people were in the camp, perhaps 10,000, perhaps fewer. The majority went to work outside the camp. Some worked in Melk others in Amstetten and so on. The largest labor brigades were those that worked on the construction of an underground factory. There they produced engines, cartridges and who knows what else. It was strenuous work. There were three shifts—morning, afternoon and night. Each individual was at work for more than twelve straight hours, and for part of the day had to be present at the roll call, or at meals. The rest of the time was spent sleeping.

The journey to the workplace was extremely difficult. Prisoners had to walk down to a railway platform built especially for them. There they waited a long time for trains, which were usually late due to frequent air raids. At the work place, on both sides of the road were powerful floodlights for the night shifts. Each day, the workers carried back dozens of their dead companions on primitive stretchers.

The medical care in Melk was appalling. It was really a so-called extermination labor camp. Only the most seriously ill, those who were dying, ever came to the infirmary. The place itself defies description. Three to four slept, suffered, and died in a single bed—and by bed I mean one section of a three-tiered bunk. The dead were taken to the crematorium, which we had a chance to thoroughly inspect when we were in Melk after liberation. Only a handful of inmates remained in the camp, and they worked extremely hard. These were invalids and the sick. They worked right in the camp. Although I remember details about life in Melk better, I do not wish to elaborate further.

I came to the gate at four o'clock just as the day shift of prisoners was leaving; they returned at five in the afternoon. At eight in the morning the night shift (which had gone to work at seven or nine the previous evening) returned, and at about midnight the afternoon shift that had left around noon came back. Often they brought back bundles of kindling wood, which they used to heat their cold quarters, or else they sold the wood to the barracks elder in exchange for soup. In other

šichtu. Jak říkám, poměry byly strašné. Ubytovací
hrozné, šatstvo nuzné, hlad veliký, práce těžké,
úmrtnost velká, bili oto.
apell byl v tělocviku
půlhodinový.
každý blockältester
měl svůj block,
kde počítal.
Já jsem stál u brány

malý komando čeká na vlak

neb seděl vedle v blocku
a běhal, kam mne blockältester posílali.
nikdy mi dali úbytek svého oběda, jinak
haus chléba, ale moc jsem z toho neměl.
v neděli byl vždy láger apell. To šli všichni
na velký appellplatz. apell přebíral raportführer
neb lagerältester a komandant. V lágru jsem
byl asi 10 dní. Když blockp. potřebovali děti,
odebrali obyčejně několika ubožákům děti, které si nesli po máce. Chudáci je všelijak ukrývali, ale slídivé oko SS

down German fighters and firing at the guards in their high towers. Sometimes the sirens had scarcely sounded as the planes swooped down out of the clouds with their regular ratatatat. The terrified guards slid down from the towers into the shelters, leaving their weapons behind. Everyone had to go to their barracks and nobody was allowed to appear outside. When explosions rumbled outside and the machine guns barked those were beautiful moments. The sound of the flak guns became weaker and weaker.[27] I crept from the gate to the nearby block—I can't remember its number—where there was a good-natured barracks elder.

It was terrible to see the deserters, mostly Russians, who in desperation tried to escape but were caught. Their punishment was frightful. They were badly beaten and then had to stand at attention day and night in front of the gate until they fell to the ground unconscious, whereupon the block commander beat and kicked them. Only when they were dead, or barely living, were they hauled to the infirmary (*Krankenstube*) where they died anyway. It was an awful sight to see those poor souls standing out there in the worst weather, at night, in the freezing cold, wearing only thin clothing, without food or drink! I was foolish at the time, but when I think about it today, I realize I might have helped them a little and alleviated their suffering, which was immense.

Sometimes, though rarely, alas, the SS did not finish their meal and gave me their bowls to wash out. I would gulp down the leftovers and then return the bowls. Their food was not outstanding but it was better than the slop we were given, although the soups in Melk were better than in Mauthausen and Auschwitz.

I got to know the SS better. Most of them were beasts, but a few were better, more kindhearted. The highest-ranking officer was very strict but just; he never punished anyone without a reason. But woe to anyone who did something wrong! I could write a lot about those moments, such as my memories of the conceited tailor from Auschwitz who sewed my buttons on in Melk, or about mates, friends, acquaintances, well-known prisoners, etc. There would be a lot to write about, but it is impossible in this brief summary.

When I think of those days I see before me the terrible suffering of the wounded and sick; the misery of poor twenty-year-old men who looked like old people, the horror, the hunger.

An Electrician's Helper

I did not see much of the boys in the block. I worked from five-thirty in the morning and returned late in the evening. The only advantage was that since my old clothes were ruined in the potato kitchen and I now performed more representative duties, I was able to get rid of my old long pants and jacket from Auschwitz, and exchange them for knickerbockers and a newer jacket. My laced boots had been stolen and I was given wooden clogs as a replacement. As a messenger who delivered messages between the SS and the prison functionaries, I was able to obtain new boots, though only with great difficulty.

I talked with Harry Osers several times. At about the same time I learned that [the electricians] disliked Zbyšek, who only made trouble and did not do any work. So I had hopes that the barracks elder would take me back, but it did not happen.

One day the Dutchman, or Belgian, from the gate regained his health and the head of the electricians took me on as his helper, I do not even remember how it happened. He was an awful man of medium height, with a cone-shaped head on a thick neck and the face of a criminal. He was a citizen of the German Reich (*Reichsdeutscher*) (i.e., a thief, a swindler or something of that sort). He had been a head electrician in Auschwitz and now was the master of a smaller workshop, where he also slept. Next-door was a room for the workers, about four Frenchmen, on his team. They were all decent chaps who did not let him walk all over them. (I do want to say more about them later on.) The work group leader (I do not remember his name. How could I, when one met so many people of different nationalities? Their names are somewhere in my sub-consciousness, but I can still see their faces in my mind's eye.) was a terrible stickler for cleanliness. As we somehow learned, he had been terribly cruel to people in Auschwitz, and he was the same here as well. He had a relative who worked outside the camp on a work detail (*Kommando*). In the evening this relative always cooked the work group

znovu a znovu, oznětujíce
německé stíhačky a stíhlá
po patech na vysokých
věžích. Někdy ani nerozmely
sirény a již se snesli zoblak
se svým pravidelným ratatata.
Posti v hroreném strachu sklonali svěří do krytů,
nechavají na koše celé své vybalení. Tenkrále musili všechni do bloků a nikdo se nesmil ukázati
venku.

Appell

25.

byly to hrozné chvíle, když venku duněly výbuchy a štěkaly kulomety. Slaběji a slaběji se ozýval flak. Také já jsem vyběhl od brány do vedlejšího bloku, nevím ani jaké měl číslo, ale byl tam docela příjemný blokový.

Strašná podívaná byla na desertéry, byli to obyčejně ruští zajatci, kteří se nechali chytit při útěku, ale byli chyceni. Jejich trest byl strašný. Hrozně zbiti museli stát v pozoru den a noc před branou, tak dlouho, dokud nepadli v bezvědomí a pak je ještě lágrslíbři bili a kopali. Teprve polomrtvé neb mrtvé je odváželi na krankenstube, kde stejně nevěděli. Byl to hrozný pohled na ty ubožáky, stojící v největším nečase, v noci v mraku již jen tak v tenkém drelu bez potravy a pití!

leader semolina because the old man apparently had something wrong with his stomach and could not tolerate the camp food.

Then I took over the work. In the morning I got up (I was still living in Block 1) and hurried to the electricians' quarters to clean, cook etc. In the evening I went back to Block 1 to sleep. I had a lot of work to do. I remember that the work group leader always found tasks for me—scrubbing the floor, peeling potatoes and polishing shoes.

As I already mentioned, those Frenchmen were great fellows. I see them all before me now and I remember what they looked like. They were pleasant, amusing guys. They often gave me potatoes and I even learned a couple of French words. But just as I forgot my Polish, I do not remember more than ten French words. The work group leader did nothing but curse and complain. These four fellows were responsible for maintaining all the electricity in Melk. There was primitive lighting in the blocks, lighting around the camp, as well as powerful searchlights. But they also repaired the lighting in the SS barracks; which was their main duty. If the officers needed work done, the work group leader himself usually went, or he sent Willi, the leader of that "famous" team. When that happened, they usually brought back something nice—cigarettes or food—and they had usually been well fed.

The electricians' workshop was five or six meters long and about three meters wide. The work group leader had a bed in the back, along with a cupboard for his things. There were also tables and shelves with various tools. In the next room were two bunks for a total of six people, and a bed on which Willi slept. There was a small stove in each room. I forgot to mention an old electrician, a Hungarian, who was very kind and had to work hard because the work group leader was angry with him. The good Frenchmen helped him out whenever they could.

I went there day in and day out, though for how long I cannot remember. It was not a pleasant life but it was a little better than in the potato kitchen. At least you could get bits of news, and every day I could watch dozens of bombers flying high over Melk and avenging the injustices committed by the Germans and their allies.

The war was coming to an end. It was about the end of March. The Russians were advancing into Austria from Hungary; the Americans were in Germany. The Germans could only last for a few months but they did not want to give up easily and above all, they did not want to simply let the prisoners go free. Then, one day, it happened.

BACK TO MAUTHAUSEN

In the Potato Kitchen Once More

There was much to talk about now, since other camps around us were being evacuated. I do not know how it came about, but one day we had to leave Block 1 and go to the back, to Block 8 or 9, above the car-repair shop. There were two blocks on each side that were former garages. This was where they housed us, the young ones from the potato kitchen, and other prisoners as well. We lived on decrepit bunks with missing planks, half-empty straw ticks and thin blankets full of holes. I had always shared a bunk with Harry Goldberger and I did so here as well. The rumor was that they would isolate us here and then, in a few days, we would most likely be sent back to Mauthausen. But nobody really knew. Why was it just we, the young ones? Did they want to get rid of us, and if so, how? We were very upset when we thought about it. Imagine, dying now when we had held out for so long! No, we had to survive!

I often prayed that my mother would survive, and I firmly believed she would. I kept telling myself that I too had to survive otherwise my mother would be very disappointed.

But nothing happened. I had to return to the potato kitchen, and ten or twenty days later we were sent back to the second floor of Block 1.

At that time I often went to see Osers, and his barracks leader wanted me back instead of Zbyšek, but we told ourselves that the war could not last much longer and we ignored the offer. I went to work in the potato kitchen every morning and came home every evening. It was unpleasant work, sitting in that humid atmosphere peeling potatoes with a primitive strip of metal, but it could not be helped; life had to go on. We put the peeled potatoes into twenty-five-liter kettles, and from there they were emptied into cauldrons. If more potatoes were needed, we worked all night. The worst of it was that the potatoes were rotten or half-rotten.

Nothing lasts forever, not even our stay in labor camp (*Arbeitslager*) Melk. True, we had expected the end to come for a long time, but when it did come it was so sudden we were all surprised and very frightened. One morning, at about ten o'clock, our barracks elder came to fetch us in the potato kitchen and ordered us to return immediately to our quarters, take our "belongings" (what did we have at that time? I had nothing . . .) and line up in the open area. At that point, everyone was given a blanket, but later we had to return it again. We each got a piece of bread and half an hour later we were lined up in the courtyard. Everyone was appalled by what we saw, which is impossible to describe. The inmates from the infirmary were also going to leave with us, and that was appalling.

A crowd of cripples and living corpses—people without legs, arms, who were seriously wounded, or had infectious diseases; all those poor beggars who were waiting for death to deliver them were herded in front of the gate and lined up in rows. The horse-drawn carts arrived and these "wounded skeletons and corpses" were counted, loaded onto the carts and taken to the railway station. Surrounded by guards, we followed behind this funeral procession. We were in a terrible mood. Where were they taking us, with those sick people? To Mauthausen? It augured nothing good. Would they gas us? It was better not to think about it.

And liberation was so near! After work we watched the town; and what joy we derived from the picture we saw! Hundreds of boats loaded with evacuees were plying their way up-stream, away from Vienna. Many freight trains loaded with soldiers and civilians were shunting back and forth on the tracks below. Where were they to go? The Russians were approaching from the east, the Americans from the west. Only a narrow strip of land remained, so where could they go?

And were we now to surrender such an opportunity and be taken instead to the German hinterland, perhaps to spend time in yet another concentration camp, and perhaps even die?

Yes, such was our situation.

Now they crammed us into closed cattle cars. Two SS climbed into every wagon and we went off into the unknown, toward new hardships.

The unknown? We soon figured out where they were taking us: back to Mauthausen! We were crushed when we crossed the bridge over the Danube and saw once more the sheer cliffs of the quarry and above it, that stone fortress, that extermination factory that caused suffering for thousands, the concentration camp called Mauthausen. At the now familiar railway station they drove us out of the cars and lined us up in rows. For the third time we walked through the town, guarded by German soldiers.

A great deal had changed here. The once proud population was now terrified, watching as military trains passed by daily, taking the army to the fast approaching front line. And what an army it was! They were mostly old men with trembling hands or unseasoned youths between the ages of thirteen and sixteen. This was what stood between them and the advancing Allies. And the air raids! The sirens wailed constantly as heavy US bombers flew over the town. Even for those people wearing red armbands with the double lightning insignia, it was no longer a laughing matter.[28]

And all those pretentious offices that we had seen in the winter were now military hospitals. All this gave us strength and reminded us of freedom. Again we walked up the steep slope to the gates, were counted, let into the camp and driven to the first barrack on the right, the showers.

THIRD CAMP

Here, in the Third Camp, in the tent camp (*Zeltlager*) and in Gunskirchen, the last and hardest phase of my imprisonment in concentration camps took place.[29] Fortunately, it ended just in time. Otherwise I would have died in a few days, like millions others, of typhus and dysentery.

Here we were again, my dear showers, for the second time. But this time it was worse. We lost all our clothes and everything else. I still had a decent coat from Auschwitz and adequate trousers, and now we had to throw it all on a heap and humbly wait our turn. Meanwhile, we watched how they killed and butchered lame horses for prisoners' soup (*Häftlingssuppe*) in the nearby kitchen.

To vše nás vlilo při vzpomínce na Svobodu.
Opět jsme těžce stoupali do vrchu k branám
KZ lágru, byli počítáni a vzpomínáni dveřmi,
příjmami a vháněni do 1 bloku v noci, ke Saúně.

————————————
————————————

Melk an der Donau je pěkné městečko se zámečkem
na vrchu (ve válce tam byl jako všude lazaret)
ale já na něj nemám pěkné vzpomínky, však
se tam ještě později vrátím.

3. TŘETÍ TÁBOR.

Zde, v 3. táboře, Zeltlagru a Gunskirchenu
se odehrávaly poslední a nejtěžší fáze mého
věznění v koncentračních táborech, které tak
tak skončily v čas, neboť nechybělo mnoho
dní a byl bych zahynul jako miliony jiných
a to na lačrní tyf a úplavici.

Tak jsme tu zase milá sauno, po druhé,
ale tentokráte to bylo horší, přišli jsme o vše
zbývající a to o všechno. Měl jsem tam ještě

When our turn came, we ran under a lukewarm shower and received torn, oversized underpants and a shirt, and that was only because a Czech was issuing the clothing and he did it as a favor to us; others were given only underpants or a shirt. Then they led us in groups of about twenty to barracks located in the rear of the Third Camp. These were the worst barracks, with only the bare floor to sleep on.

Some boys were assigned to Block 29; we were sent to Block 30. In this camp, which was somewhat lower down than the others, there were five barracks. In Block 29, the barracks elder was our former head prisoner from the men's camp in Birkenau.

They actually divided us into two groups. Those in Block 29 were somewhat better off; in Block 30 we had an impossible barracks elder, the worst in the entire camp, I think. He beat and kicked us at every opportunity. He was a brute and a criminal, a citizen of the Reich from Germany. He lived in "luxury." He exchanged our bread and margarine rations for good meals for himself; he stole from us whenever he could, and that allowed him to live agreeably. He was also well dressed and so in fact he lacked nothing.

In the evening some prisoners spread blankets on the shining floor so as not to make it dirty, and put down straw mattresses. The floor was polished daily. We were not allowed to wear shoes inside the barracks, but carried them in our hands. When it rained, they drove us inside where we sat on the bare floor; sometimes they left us outside in the rain. In the evening they drove us inside with whips; then, using kicks and clubs, they forced us to lie down on our side as close to each other as possible so that everyone would fit in. I had never seen such brutes before.

From our previous stay, I remembered the Czechs in Block 21 and so I went looking for Míša Grünwald, who was in Block 29. We walked to the gate together, but of course we were unable to go out. Franta—who was head of the maintenance team and the recognized leader of all the Czechs imprisoned at that time in Mauthausen—was in the adjoining second camp.[30] There was a round hole in the wall separating the second and third camps, probably made for a water pipe, and the prisoners of the two camps could talk to each other through it. And it was in this way, after a great effort, that we were able to ask a prisoner to go to Block 21. Franta was not there but someone else came and said he would send Franta to us. Franta came the next day, gave each of us a piece of bread, and was very kind to us. He promised to come again soon and keep an eye out for us.

Another day went by. At noon, a half liter of impossible soup that was so bad it made us vomit; in the evening, we were given a spoonful of moldy bread crumbs and a blow with a club sent us to bed. If anyone needed to go to the toilet at night (if he had diarrhea) he usually could not get out of the room because there were no spaces between the sleeping bodies. If he did manage to get out, the space where he had been sleeping was usually gone and he had nowhere to lie down again when he returned. In the morning they woke us by beating us with rubber hoses. We had to stand outside all day or sit in the mud and watch the misery and the horrible theatre around us, such as prisoners doing the difficult exercises ordered by the SS to punish them—something called "*Sport.*" Prisoners had to run in a circle and when ordered, lie on the ground, and then get up and run again, and this went on and on. Anyone who did not fall down or get up quickly enough was beaten and trampled on by the heavy boots of the SS. One morning when I did not run fast enough from the barrack, I too received a heavy blow to my head.

And washing—once in a while they chased us into the wash rooms (*Waschräume*), where we had to take off our clothes and wash under cold water. We had to put our dirty clothes back on again while we were still wet.

The question was: What would become of us? After all, we were in a transit camp. There were rumors about a tent camp, horrible and frightening rumors about death, starvation, thirst, heat, and cold; about a camp to which all Jews would be sent to die of hunger and disease.

Franta had not been to see us for a long time, so we sent him a message. He had had a disagreement with our barracks elder and had beaten him up. It took several days for a response. Franta sent a friend, who took us to the main camp. Franta was waiting for us there and took us to the prisoner who served as camp secretary (*Lagerschreiber*)

podlahu vždy na bok a barabka donutili
lehnout co nejblíže k sobě, aby se do bloku všechni
vešli. Takové surovce jsem ještě neviděl vůbec.

Vzpomněl jsem si opět na
ty čechy na bloku 21 a proto jsem
vyhledal Mirka grünwaldového, který
byl na bl. 29. Šli jsme spolu
k braně, ale samozřejmé je, že jsme
se nedostali ven. Franta byl vedle na 2
táboře vrchní stubendienst a uznávaná hlava
všech Čechů, vězněných tehdy v Mauthausenu. Vzadu byla mezi 2.-3. lágrem kulatá
díra, ani na vodu, kudy spolu vězňové
a těchto táborů hleděli. A tak i my
po dlouhé námaze jsme požádali jednoho
vězně a ten došel na bl 21. Franta
tam nebyl, přišel však jiný, který
nám řekl, že Frantu za námi pošle.

44

and to other barracks where he had friends. He told us there were several Jewish boys posing as Arians. Franta persuaded the secretary to register them under a different religion and for that reason they did not have to go to the tent camp but instead were able to stay here and do various small jobs. It was a beautiful idea, but it did not work. The secretary refused to do it for us. Disappointed, we wandered back to the Third Camp and never saw Franta again. He was a good man and he had done all he could.

Then it became a certainty—an exact deadline. The barracks elder put us on a list, lined us up, and ordered the Poles to take our better shoes and give us worse ones. We resisted but we were helpless against the blows of the maintenance team. They stripped us of our last decent clothing and next day, they lined us up. We were in a hopeless condition. At that time I had two numbers on my arm: the tattoo from Auschwitz and the Mauthausen number on a metal plate that was valid here.

We went out of the same gate again—the fourth time I had gone this way. Outside the camp, work details were dragging rocks; there was shouting everywhere, the sound of blows, and desperate screams. An escort of the German army (*Wehrmacht*), or perhaps it was the state police (*Staatspolizei*), surrounded us. We walked beside barbed wires, barracks, guards and machine guns, down to a fenced hillside behind a garbage dump to a rather steep slope with five large circus-like tents in the shape of an "A." The guards stood back, a primitive gate opened and we were driven inside. So here you are; the gate closed.—"Do what you want here, you damned Jews!"

TENT CAMP

Now what? We stood there helplessly, looking around. Here stood several empty soup barrels, there a heap of corpses, over there lay several prisoners, and past that, a guard walking up and down. A man hurried toward us, registered us, and led us to the third tent. This was where we would live, though who knew for how long. We went out to look around. Look! There was a boy we knew from somewhere. Yes, he had come from Auschwitz and had been here almost a month—a month in this hell. But still he was better off. He had a friend in the upper camp, who brought him bread and salami, which no one here had. He slept in a sort of shack near the gate. He promised to give us a tarp, and he kept his word. Still, he was not a good fellow, but rather a show-off who hit others and harassed them.

He told us about the horrible conditions here. He said that not long ago there were so many people here that they had to sleep outside on the ground and even so, there was not enough room. A bomb had fallen on this encampment (possibly dropped by the Germans themselves). It had killed many people, and then they cooked human flesh. Brrr!

Where had all those people gone?

Somewhere to Wels, but I did not know where that was.[31] We were supposed to follow them soon, or so the camp commander (*Lagerführer*), a terrible guy who had recently shot someone here, told us.

Who was in this camp? Mainly Hungarian Jews who had come directly from fighting the Russians, or from their homes, and so they were not yet as run-down and hungry. The SS came here in secret to trade bread for smuggled jewelry, and there were also a few good-look-ing girls here. The Hungarians also had rucksacks filled with clothing and blankets.

Some of these things we only heard about; others we saw ourselves.

I do not know how long we were there; perhaps about fourteen days. But it was worse than before. At night, about eight of us lay on the muddy ground, covered by a thin tarp. The poorly erected tent did not protect us from the strong wind or the rain. The entire camp was on a slope and water from the spring downpours passed directly through our tents. Half the area covered by the tent was under water and we had to huddle together even more tightly. Human bodies were entwined in various ways in the drier part of the tent. Only the soli-darity of us Czech boys, though we were few, protected us from the stronger Hungarians, who were a great majority in the camp. Here too people were constantly dying, with no medical help, and were pushed aside by healthier inmates. It was a hard struggle for us, but we survived, all except one Austrian friend, who was dragged off to the tent for the dying.

Food, yes, food, the thing that was supposed to keep us alive. What had changed for us? For one thing, we got much less, if that were possible. Instead of half a liter of the miserable liquid they called turnip soup, we got (if there was any left) only a quarter liter and we no longer got the spoonful of moldy breadcrumbs.

The rumors were terrible! Several times, the Hungarian leaders reported that the war was over, that Hitler had died, that the Germans had surrendered.

Was there any truth in it? Perhaps it was true that Hitler had died, but otherwise? Perhaps it gave us courage to live on, but what encouraged us most were the daily flights of American bombers rumbling darkly above us. Now there were air raids even during the day. I remember one in particular. Bombs were falling in the distance; we could hear explosions. We could hear the sound of the flak guns getting closer, and then airplanes flew over us. One bomber was hit, and what seemed like little clouds descended from the air. At first we did not know what they were. Then we understood. Above the woods, not far from the camp, four parachutes came down; it was the crew of the stricken airplane, American soldiers, the cost of the air raids. Immediately, the Germans rushed out to the woods; we heard shooting and then silence. Later we learned that all four had been shot in the Mauthausen concentration camp.

Again there was talk that we would be leaving, and it was known where we would be going: Wels, the place where the first Hungarians had gone a month ago. Who knew what it would be like there? They said it was a large camp—ten thousand people. Some said the Red Cross was there and would hand us over to the Americans. The pessimists said there were gas chambers. Nobody knew any more.

But one morning we got up and hurried to the lower gate, where they let us out in groups of one hundred, escorted by the local police (*Schutzpolizei*).[32] These were all Austrians, somewhat more reasonable people than the fanatical SS.

The camp looked awful—corpses and more corpses, the groaning of the sick, ragged clothing, the filth and the stench.

We arrived at the gate; one hundred of us. Four guards—"Get going!" (*Los!*)—on we went.

GUNSKIRCHEN

It was probably April 28th when we dragged ourselves along, in terrible shoes with nails sticking into our feet, through the heat, past the quarries—the dreaded Mauthausen quarries! How many camps had we seen here, how many prisoners lugging rocks? What was our destination? Wels!

Walking Again

It was noon when we trudged again through the small town of Mauthausen. What did it look like now? It looked like everywhere else we had passed through—ragged soldiers, volunteer guards, more soldiers, camouflaged vehicles, horses and tanks. Most were members of the German army air force (*Wehrmacht Luft*). We waited a while on one side of a railway bridge across the Danube. Then, in groups of one hundred, we crossed to the other bank and then marched on through small villages and towns. The heat was terrible, and we were scarcely given time to rest. Then chaos set in; the groups of one hundred got mixed up and formations fell apart. Yet, with soldiers everywhere, there was no thought of escape.

We pressed forward through the heat, in our bad shoes. The guards, too, were tired because they were all elderly members of the local police, mainly Viennese. They talked to us and were quite pleasant. The leader of the entire transport kept coming by, urging us to walk faster. There were SS troops in the rear who occasionally shot the poor stragglers who could go no further.

I remember that journey quite vividly, the villages teeming with soldiers, the ridiculous youngsters in uniforms, the tanks, the artillery, the vehicles, the exhausted lines of prisoners in striped uniforms. At every water pump we greedily gulped down cold water. And on we went!

The many places we passed through, the many stories and events that happened, are engraved in my memory. We walked on, even when the entire landscape became shrouded in darkness and the moon popped into the sky. On we went!

It was about eleven o'clock at night when the procession slowly came to a halt and we waited on the road for our turn to get food. The food was not bad. Soup and a piece of bread with margarine, something we hadn't seen for a long time.

It was dark everywhere. The field kitchens had probably been set up in a large farm. Then they herded us to a fenced meadow where we lay down in the wet grass and, in spite of the cold and dampness, we soon gave in to sleep. After all, we were exhausted!

We were on our way again before the sun was up. The field kitchens went ahead of us so we would have some soup in the evening. At noon we received a small piece of bread.

On and on we walked. We spent the next night in Weißkirchen; again, we slept in a meadow near a small forest. In the evening we got soup, in the morning a piece of bread, then we continued walking for the third day. It started to rain, to pour! The pace quickened. The march required our last remaining energy. Wels. From the hilltop, as we approached the town, it looked fairly large. Everywhere there were encampments with Red Cross military field hospitals and destroyed houses. We crossed a long bridge over a filthy river. It rained steadily. We walked through the town and kept on going. Where were they taking us? We left the town and walked on. When would this march end? We were looking forward now to at least some decent accommodation where we could dry out, receive food and sleep in comfort after the difficult, exhausting march. Not many from the tent camp had made it this far. How many lay dead among the tents, how many had died along the road to this place, and how many were still dropping dead on the muddy road?

We turned off the road onto a muddy path into the woods.

Disappointment

It was still raining. We were drenched to the bone. We staggered through puddles and mud on a path through a dense forest. Here and there was a primitive cabin, with tanks and soldiers standing nearby. There were even airplanes hidden here. The forest began to thin out. We approached log cabins surrounded by guards. Was this supposed to be a camp? It was awful! They herded us into those cabins, which had earthen floors. In this airless space (there were only tiny windows) we lay without blankets on the bare floor, in our soaked rags. Was this the camp? Impossible! Crowded together, we sat on the bare floor. Soon we fell asleep—without food, soaked, terribly disappointed.

Yes, this was the camp of the dead, forgotten among the trees of a dense forest, without air and without sun. Huge puddles surrounded the barracks. In the back, a primitive latrine, that was all.

There were Hungarians everywhere. They fought and quarreled; a terrible scum.

Our hopes for a better camp vanished. Shouting awakened us. We went outside for the morning roll call among the trees. Our teeth were chattering with the cold. I stood there with Míša Grünwald under a wet, torn blanket. We were both ill and we were beginning to lose hope of surviving, yet so near the end!

The memory of my mother commanded me to endure. I thought she would surely survive and that without me she would not be happy. Endure!

These were terrible, hopeless moments in the forest, among the puddles, where the sun did not shine and where even in summer it was cold. This went on for ten days—ten terrible days.

The nights were awful, and so were the days. By day we either sat in the barracks (our place was at the entrance, so that everyone coming and going kicked and shoved us) or staggered through puddles in that little piece of forest. And at night! No one could sleep on this narrow piece of ground, on this wet earth, with nothing to cover us. We trembled with cold. There was not enough room. Anyone who was sicker than the others was thrown out into the rain where, unable to move, he would die within a few days, or would drown after having been thrown into a puddle. That's how terrible it was there. Several times during the night, these poor wretches were tossed out over our heads. I remember that Harry Kraus wanted to take the shoes off one of them.[33]

It was hopeless. We wept from the hopelessness, the cold and the hunger. The pouring rain soaked everything, and the sun never shone.

Red Cross Parcels

What kind of food did we get? Once a day, we got a little soup, no more. Otherwise nobody cared for us. Several times a day the SS would drive out the stronger men by hitting them or firing their guns, to bury the hundreds of corpses.

There was no water here. For several thousand people, only a single demijohn of water was brought daily. It wasn't even enough for drinking! Everybody had lice crawling over their bodies. It was awful.

I could only pray and hope. That was my defense. The memory of my mother strengthened me; the memory of my father told me to survive and take revenge.

Then something happened that was the most crushing of all, mentally: the arrival of parcels from the Red Cross. They were meant for all the children up to the age of fifteen.

They were to be handed out the next day.

We rushed to the kitchen. But the SS confiscated the parcels and only a few fortunate ones managed to take some food away, but they became sick after eating the delicacies. One of them, a Slovak boy, slept with us. He was so sick he had to lie down the whole time and had terrible diarrhea. It was really foolish. For weeks he had hardly eaten anything and now he was drinking condensed milk and eating chocolate.

We waited to get the parcels but our turn never came. I cannot describe the awful moments, the terrible craving for something sweet, and the hunger. I cannot describe it. You have to experience it yourself to possibly understand it. Some were driven mad and kept going to the kitchen. Some of them were shot; others were beaten up.

THE BIG DAY—MAY 7th, 1945—LIBERATION

Each day, the sound of shooting got stronger and drew nearer.[34] How much longer would it be before they reached us? The American troops would probably be the first to reach us but when, when would that be?

The terrible Hungarians would probably beat us to death, destroy us, and kill us. I would hate them to the end of my days, just as I would hate those awful Polish Jews or the Carpathian-Russians! They were all the same!

One evening they brought us news that the Germans had left. Based on our experiences from the tent camp, we did not believe it. And sure enough, it was not true. But we did live to see it. By the following evening it was certain. The SS had left in a car with a white flag. The date was May 6, 1945. (Of course we didn't know the precise date at the time.)

There was jubilation and joy, but it was subdued. There were only a few who could still move. Those who could threw themselves into the kitchen and fought for the remaining bits of food. They fought amongst themselves and even threatened each other with weapons left behind by the Germans. It was both beautiful and awful.

Free! Thank God! We had made it! Thoughts and memories of those horrible years, and memories of our friends swirled through our minds. One of us brought a loaf of bread. We ate a little bit. Then friends from the next barrack came. They had a piece of horsemeat. We discussed what to do with it. It was getting dark. Many people were leaving the camp. We decided to stay one more night.

I could not fall asleep for a long time. I thought about my fate and remembered my parents. But then I slept well. After all, we were free.

Early next morning we went behind the barrack, roasted the piece of meat and took it along with us. We walked past abandoned barracks. There was litter everywhere, evidence of a hasty flight. We found a bicycle, which Fink rode.[35] It had no tires. With some difficulty, we dragged ourselves through the woods. There were prisoners everywhere, walking with us. And then, look! Over there, on the road—we saw our first American soldier.

While we were in Gunskirchen, cut off from the world, the American armies had swept deeper into Austria. But they only entered Wels on May 7th. It was the last day of World War Two in Europe.[36] We could not have survived much longer. I had typhus, though I was unaware of it at the time. I only rejoiced that the war was over and I staggered on.

1. část.	—	Pod ochranou a péčí Americké Armády.
2. část.		Na území Rudé armády.
3. část.		Ve vlasti. (Zase v republice)

IV. díl.

69

IV

POST-WAR HARDSHIPS

Under the Care of the US Army

HÖRSCHING

Meeting with Americans, First Meal

We rushed onto the road. So that is what American soldiers look like! He was the first human being we met after our release from bondage, and moreover, he was a liberator. He had just stopped a motorcycle with a German officer in the sidecar. He tried to take away the officer's weapon, but the officer took out some kind of document and continued on his way. We were very surprised.[37]

We walked on after the others. Several cottages stood near the road. We headed for them. There was a pump, and we drank water from it. A farmer bought the bicycle from us for a loaf of bread and some lard. It was our first meal. Each of us had a slice, then we continued on our way. We passed soldiers who waved to us and threw us candy. There were Czechs among them. Some of them took pictures of us. They were nice young men. They rested by the side of roads, wearing all their gear. The most beautiful sight were the endless convoys of cars and tanks streaming on all the better roads. It was nice to see the tanks with black soldiers sitting on top; a beautiful, well-organized army.

They told us to keep straight on to the next village, where there was a food depot and we could eat our fill. And so we dragged ourselves on. Everywhere we saw smartly dressed soldiers with neatly pressed pants, eating chocolate and smoking.

Past us streamed endless lines of tanks and lorries carrying provisions. We were entering a village, a long and drawn-out settlement. Everywhere there were peasant carts loaded with crates and canned food. Where had they gotten it from? Everyone carried away bags and baskets full of provisions. In front of a large single-storey building we could see a throng of former prisoners. Then we saw that it was a warehouse, full of German army provisions.

The Food Storehouse and the Journey to the Hospital

We decided that it was not worthwhile forcing our way through the crowd, so we walked on a little further, where we saw an unfinished garage without a roof. We decided to stay there for the day. We gathered up some bricks and wood and made a fire. Some of us went to the storehouse to fetch food. What a sight! There were piles of sacks and crates full of oats, corn, peas, and flour. The soldiers gave everyone what they wanted. It was a sort of army warehouse, a reserve of last resort. There was even canned meat and sugar. The farmers took away carts loaded with sacks and crates of cans. They would have enough food to last them many years.

We heated up the cans. Oats with sugar was the best. Some very quickly became sick, and everyone had diarrhea, which made quite a mess! In the afternoon we went to the surrounding villages to hunt for bread. In some places they gave us soup as well. In the evening it threatened to rain. We hid the remaining food and went to the warehouse to sleep on piles of sacks. By this time, however, there were not many sacks left and the more sought-after food like sugar, oats and canned goods had all been taken away. We all became sick and had to go to the toilet constantly.

During the night the rain stopped. In the morning we trudged on; we walked to the highway. Some of us were already there when a truck stopped. The men in the truck shouted to us to hurry up and said they would take us to the station. It was hard for us to run, and I could not keep up. I was dizzy and was the last to arrive. The truck was already moving when they pulled me aboard. They were Frenchmen. They took us through Wels, where we got fuel and drove on.

There was destruction everywhere; there were many soldiers and American vehicles. Airplanes circled over our heads. I felt unwell. Soon we arrived at some large buildings. They were barracks belonging to the former German army air force. This was where they were bringing survivors from the concentration camps, mainly Jews. The truck stopped. We got off and lay down on the grass. Someone went to fetch water and they brought back books as well. Then they assigned us to a room on the first floor, but we had to carry the bunks up to the room ourselves. I couldn't manage. I collapsed, feeling terribly ill. My friends first thought I was pretending, but then they saw that I was not, that I was really sick.

The Hospital

That evening I tried to go to the toilet, but I collapsed again. I did not know what was wrong with me. They helped me to the toilet but I didn't feel any better. Harry was also very sick. The others put up the bunks and got ready for the night. That afternoon I slept for a while. Then someone went to ask what should be done with the sick. Shortly afterward I was taken to the hospital.

There they were just getting organized, so I had to go to the attic. They laid me down among the others on straw bedding, gave me two packages of biscuits and that was it. My friends left and I had an awful night. All I wanted was water, and someone next to me who was able to walk had a bottle and gave it to me in exchange for biscuits. Around noon the next day they carried me downstairs, took off my clothes, burnt them, and disinfected me with some sort of powder. Then they gave me some underwear and carried me to the second floor where they put me in a room on the lower bunk. The caregivers were captured medics, who gave us sheets and blankets in slipcovers. Everything was very nice.

Then, I more or less lost track of myself for a week. I sat on the toilet all the time while the healthier patients helped me, and ate my food. They said they were wonderful delicacies, the best food and drink. One woman brought me cold tea; it was my only nourishment. I was delirious and kept calling out for my mother. No one thought I would survive. There were about eight of us in the room.

I gradually got better, but the food got worse. When good food was available, I could not eat it; now when I could eat, it was worse. But it didn't matter—after years of suffering it felt like the royal treatment.

I do not remember all the details, but in any case, it is not so important.

Several Hungarian and Polish Jews lived there with me. They were constantly arguing with each other. Two of them died and one was taken to the infectious ward. Through the window, and using a rope, they bartered cigarettes for various kinds of food and carried on silly conversations with the German orderlies. I was the only one who knew some English and soon all the doctors and nurses of the American army on our floor came to visit me. They were good people: Dr. Filtzer and nurses Kokoruda and Ormes.[38] They brought me chocolate and American newspapers. They visited every day. They often talked with me and told me about the USA and other interesting matters. When they were leaving they gave me their addresses and we later corresponded.

Once I received a transfusion of two liters of blood. Then I got stronger and was able to walk around the room. Those were moments of uncertainty and hope. Was my mother alive? Everyone tried to reassure me, and I came to believe that she had returned. Then they moved me to another room and my (new American) friends left. They were all looking forward to going back home to their families. The nurse called Kukoruda was apparently of Czech ancestry, though he had been born in the USA.

At that time I learned (through the window) that the rest of the boys were somewhere near the airfield that had previously belonged to the air force (*Luftwaffe*) and was now in American hands. Some of the boys, like Harry and Gorilla, were also in the hospital.[39]

After some time I was able to walk up and down the corridor, and once I even went down to the yard. But I was still weak and soon had to come back. Then we were issued trousers and coats.

Somewhere I got hold of a pencil and a stack of paper and I began to draw, especially maps of towns.

First Outings and Meeting Friends

After I had been in the hospital about five weeks, I went to the airfield. There were jeeps with black soldiers everywhere and they drove like lunatics. I walked slowly through their tent encampment. Everywhere entertainment and games were in progress. They amused themselves in all kinds of ways and the main thing was, they were quite cheerful! I went right to the back where there were piles of crates containing food that the bombers were constantly bringing in. I asked about my friends but nobody knew anything. I returned to the hospital. The next day I visited Harry.

One day I traded my shoes for a piece of bread and three eggs. I already had a good appetite but the doctors were cautious and did not give us too much to eat.

I went to the airport for a second time. And this time I found them. They were all there; only Gorila had apparently gone a little crazy and was taken away. They were fairly well off. They stole food parcels at the airport and so had plenty of everything. Chaim had even started a collection of cartridges.

I started going to the airport frequently. As my friends and I talked, I learned that the Polish boys had caught the leader (*Lagerführer*) of the tent camp when he came to clean their room. They recognized him and accused him of belonging to the SS, which the Americans did not know, and began to beat him with chairs. But the guards intervened and took him away. Apparently there were other such discoveries.

Several times, when looking out the window, I saw a Czech car marked "ČSR." They were arranging to come and take their people away.

At that time we got parcels from the British Red Cross with toilet articles, which were very useful.

From the window, I liked watching the changing of the guard, which was done in jeeps, or the columns of cars and tanks driving back and forth between the surrounding garrisons and the airfield.

One day Mr. Grünwald came to the camp to pick up Míša. He had learned about him from a Czech officer. Next day he left with him in a military car. The boys got hold of fuel for him.

It was rumored that we would be going home soon. The healthy Czechs were already signed up. A woman, probably from the American Joint Distribution Committee, visited them.

One afternoon I went to visit my friends again. They were ready to leave. They told me to come with them; otherwise I would get stuck here. Gorila was leaving as well. So I ran as fast as I could to the hospital, took my toilet articles and returned. Soon trucks arrived and we boarded. There were about five hundred of us Czechs and Slovaks, but mostly Jews from Carpathian Ruthenia.

And so, in fact, I ran away from the hospital. Only Harry Kraus stayed there. He somehow got home via Budapest. So we went off to Linz, where they said we might stay for a few days and then on—home, to our native land.

Was my mother alive? That was my main worry, and my main hope.

These were the really critical moments of my life. How many of us had survived? We, the young Czechs—there were maybe ten of us—maybe more. Who knows? There were awfully few of us.

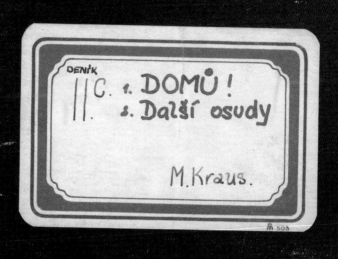

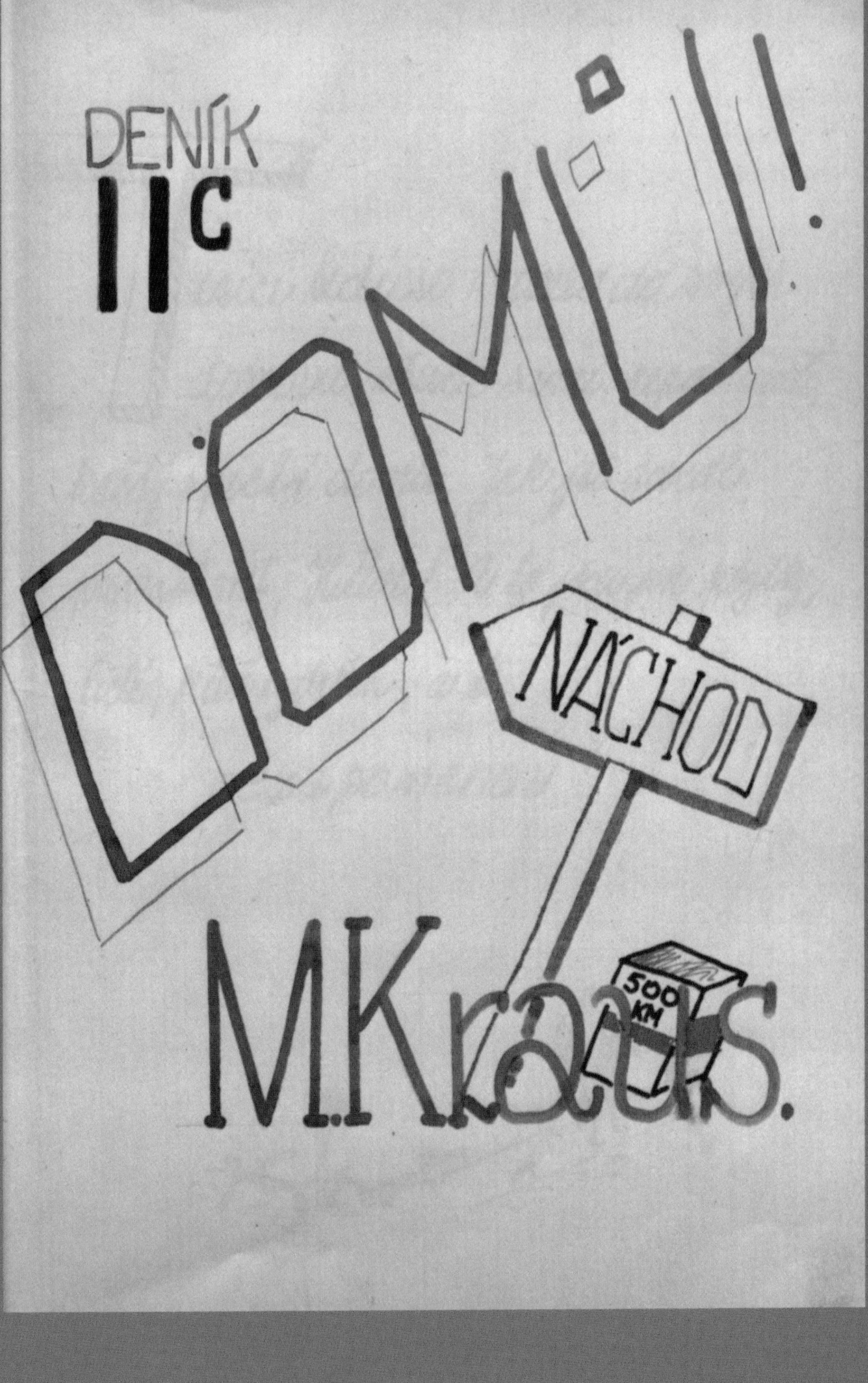
DENÍK
IIc
DOMŮ!
NÁCHOD
500 KM
M.K.

Tisíce lidí se vracelo do svých domovů, všude samí repatrianti, každý spěchá domů. Jak jsi dovedl převrátit svět, Hitlere! A to jsou jen zbytky, lidé, kteří vydrželi, a ti

nezapomenou!

Journey Home

Náchod—500km
Psáno, A.D. 1947, in my own hand

Thousands of people returned to their homes, repatriates were everywhere. Everyone was in a hurry to get home. How you turned the world upside down, Hitler! And these were mere remnants—people who endured and who

SHALL NOT FORGET!

Památce
svých rodičů.

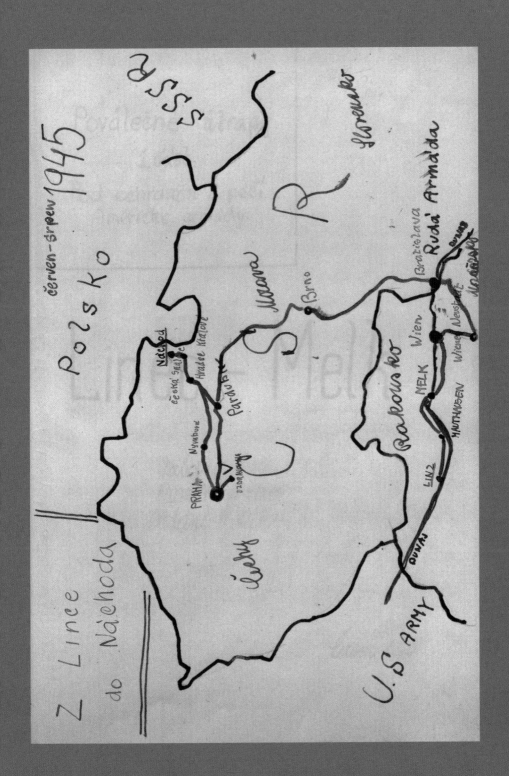

1, Tábor v Linci.

Motory aut spokojeně bručí, blížíme se
k městu. Všude u silnice jsou rozbitá auta, ale
míjíme také prostranství, kde jsou stovky rozkří-
žených aut, buď německých neb americkych.
Nejsou v pořadu. Vítěz má dost svých, v těch
dne má tolik, že i ty rozbíjejí.

Vjíždíme do trosek města. Žádný dům
není celý. Několik ulice jsou zataraseny
a leží v troskách. Západní letci ji pěkně zřídili.

Opět nás vraželi do tábora, bývalý koncentrák
ruskych zajatců. Několik dřevěných baráků a bláto.

Vylézáme. Jsou tu již nějací lidé ubytováni. Přibíhá
nějaký člověk a ukazuje kam máme jít.
Opět se spí na podlaze, ale úplně.
Bez dek – ale po hřeji nás pocit
svobody a tak nám to tě
tak nevadí. Jsem ještě hodně

6

CAMP IN LINZ

The car engines hummed contentedly as we approached a town. Wrecked vehicles lined the road; yet we also passed open fields where there were hundreds of undamaged cars, German or American. They were not in use. The victor had enough vehicles of his own. These were superfluous.

We entered the ruined town. Not a single house was left undamaged. Some streets were blocked and lay in ruins. The Western airmen had done a nice job.

They took us to another camp, a former [German] concentration camp for Russian prisoners of war. It comprised several wooden barracks surrounded by mud. We got out. Some people were living here already. A man came running up and showed us where to go. Again, we slept on the floor, without blankets, but the feeling of freedom kept us warm and we did not mind it as much. I was still weakened from the hospital, where I really should have stayed. There were about ten of us, all boys. Some had food and cigarettes (though they did not smoke). I had only my toilet kit but it was enough for me.

It rained again. In the evening they loaded us on Studebaker trucks and took us through the ruins of the town to a large building, that was not too badly damaged.[40] There we undressed and were disinfected with some sort of powder. Then we were driven back. Near the gate stood a truck; Gorila was on it. Apparently he had changed his mind and would return to Hörsching.

We registered on large sheets of paper. Then we were formed into groups of twenty. We stayed in that camp for about two days. Nothing special happened to us there. On the third day large trucks arrived and we climbed aboard in our designated groups. It was quite crowded. At the last minute, Gorila appeared from somewhere and climbed onto the truck. He seemed to have gone somewhat crazy and the boys avoided him, saying he was dangerous. Near the gate everyone got a ration of food for the trip. Because Gorila was not registered, he got nothing. However, the boys who had provisions gave him some.

We drove through the town again, but this time we took the main streets, which brought us to the harbor. There we got out, walked across a narrow gangway and boarded a nice steamboat.

neslábly z té nemocnice, kde jsme vlastně měli ještě
zůstat. Je nás ar 10 chlapců. Někteří mají s sebou
trochu jídla a cigarety (ač nekouří). Já mám jen
své mycí potřeby, ale to mi stačí.

    A opět pěšo. Večer nás nakládají na Studebakry
a vezou přes teměř město do nějaké velké budovy, která
není ani moc poškozená. Tam se svlékneme a jsme
desinfikováni nějakým práškem. Pak jdeme zpět.
V bráně stojí nějaký náklaďák a v něm jídla. My si
to rozmyslila a pojede zpět do Hoeschlingu.

    Registrujeme se na takové archy. Jako trošíme
party ar 20 ti členné. V tom táboře jsme byli ar dva
dny. Nic rob. se nám zde nepřihodilo. Asi třetího dne
ráno přijela velká nákladní auta a po partách

jsme nasedali.
Napresovaní jsme
byli pěkně. V poslední
chvíli se odněkud vzal
gorila a lezl do auta. Byl

celý nějaký pobláznený a kluci se ho stranili, říkali, že
je nebezpečný. V bráně dostal každý jedno ration na
cestu. Jelikož přišla nebýt zapráv, tak na něj víc
nezbylo, ale kluci, co měli u sebe zásoby, mu něco dali.

    Opět jsme projížděli městem, ale nyní hlavními
ulicemi. Vezli nás k přístavu. Tam jsme vylezli
a po takové lávce jsme šedli na docela pěkný parní-
ček.

    2., Parníkem po Dunaji.

    Nacpali nás dolů do podpalubí, takže jsme
zatím ta lidi nic neviděli. Musila to být pěkná loď

8

nyní však, když se jí používalo se přepravě tolika
osob, byla dosti poškozená, hlavně vnitřní zařízení.
Viděli jsme však také několik hezdrně zařízených
pokojů.

Zde jsme se tedy usadili, otevřeli si
balíčky jídla a pojídali. Později jsme vyšli ven
na palubu a pozorovali krajinu. Bylo dosud pěkné
počasí. Několikrát jsme potkali ruský hlídkový
člun s děli. To jsme již byli v území, kde byla
okupační armáda ruská.

Na palubě byli asi 3 američtí vojáci a
jeden ruský důstojník. Ale lidi, ten rozdíl.
Ten rus vypadal jako nějaký tulák nebo metař.
Američani měli pěkné pušky na kalhotech a vypa-
dali jako a velkoměsta. No poznat se to
nedalo, a to byl př-ce důstojník a oni
obyčejní vojáci!

WIENA

9

BY STEAMBOAT ON THE DANUBE

They crammed us into the lower deck, so we saw nothing of the boat. It must have been a nice boat once, but now, after they used it to transport so many people, it was considerably damaged, especially the interior furnishings. Nevertheless, we also saw a few beautifully furnished cabins.

We settled down, opened our food parcels, and started to eat. Later we climbed up on deck and watched the landscape. The weather was quite nice. Several times we encountered a Russian patrol boat armed with cannons. We were already in the zone occupied by the Russian army. On deck were three American soldiers and one Russian officer. But boy, what a difference! The Russian looked like a tramp or a street sweeper. The Americans had neatly pressed pants and looked like they came from a large city. There was no comparison, even though the Russian was an officer and the Americans were ordinary soldiers! Then someone brought some water and we made cold bouillon from the packets of instant soup. It was quite refreshing.

Then, in the distance, on a steep slope we saw a fortress, towers, stone quarries. We were approaching Mauthausen, the infamous concentration camp. Were the Germans still there? Again, we saw the town pressed against the rock. We took off our caps and looked sadly at those rocks and for a long time, we talked about that terrible camp. Then we came to Ybbs, and soon we were passing between the hills on either side of the Danube. We caught a glimpse of the Melk abbey, then the town appeared. The Danube is very wide here, with several tributaries. Taking one of them, we approached the jetty at Melk, where several ships were tied up, along with a Russian boat, heavily armed, with a strange, rag-tag crew.

část 2.

Na území
Rudé armády.

MELK - WIENER NEUSTADT -
- BRATISLAVA.

On Red Army Territory

TRANSFER IN MELK

We walked down the gangway, and for a while they left us waiting on the shore. Then several ragged-looking soldiers with medals began to line us up and count us. Eventually, other soldiers appeared from a building that was flying an American flag, handed us over, and then got into a jeep and drove off. We walked a little further into the town but had to wait there for the remnants of the Russian army, as this group of dirty faces called themselves, were on their way home, or else heading out to plunder another region. In front were several of their dilapidated cars, followed by American Studebakers and cannon. The Russians shouted and sang. That lasted about twenty minutes and we were able to continue. As before, we took the same route up to the camp where we had spent so many terrible weeks.

By now, there were only Russians here. Refugees and former prisoners were plundering the region. The population, mainly women, had fled to the American zone.

Instead of an SS guard, a shabby fellow with a rifle stood at the gate. They led us inside. Acquaintances from other camps shouted at us from the windows. They took us to a barrack in the middle of the camp near the open area, gave us bread and margarine and then left. How long would we be here? Around us there were only Russians from the camps. We were afraid.

We were not allowed to leave the camp. Instead of the SS, there were Red Army guards here. But at least the atmosphere was happier. They cooked a fairly good soup (of course there were no American delicacies). The Russians were kindhearted, but they did not fuss over us. The next day we went to another barrack, made our beds on the bunks and waited to see what would happen to us, and when we would leave. Some people had been waiting here for two weeks.

We now explored the camp as much as we were allowed to, including the crematorium. There was plenty to see. We saw an ingenious oven, a cellar for drowning victims alive and other devices.

s námi bude dít, kdy odjedeme.
Někteří zde čekali již také
14 dní.

Prohlédli jsme si nyní důkladně tábor, neboť jsme
všude mohli. Také krematorium. Bylo zde co
prohlížet. Úmyslná pec, sklepení k utlpění
objeti za živa a jiné příštroje.

Po několika dnech nás ráno vzbudili a šlo
se dolů na nádraží. Nejdříve jsme myslili, že
pojedeme auty, kterých stálo asi 30 na prostoru
(samozřejmě že, že to byly Studebakery.) a tak jsme
se rozloučili i s tímto táborem a putovali dále,
s všelijakými myšlenkami.

2. Cesta vlakem.

Tak jsme zase tady, na tom nádraží a
za chvíli lezeme do vagonů, ale do osobních,
ne už do nákladáků.

14

Jsme tam sice pěkně maplováni, ale přeci vidíme.
Všude plno rusů, mužů i žen. Také vedle nás je řada
nárazadel, na němž sedí nějaký mladší nespořádaný
rus, který má ruce stále pod sukní své partnerky,
narvavé, veselé Rusky.

A za chvíli (asi 2 hod) se jede. Pomalu, velmi
pomalu, ale přeci. Všude jsou potrhané kolejnice,
primitivní mosty a tak se jede opatrně.

Míjíme rozbitá města, všude rozbité mosty
a vykolejené vlaky, rozstřílená auta i lokomotivy.

Pak nikdo přijde a hlásí, že až vlak zase
zastaví, má z každé skupiny jít někdo
pro chleba a margarín do voního nákladního
vagonu. Tři kluci od nás již čistí zastávce
vylezají a hrnou se do předu. Je tam už pěkná
pranta. Ale než přijdou na řadu, vlak se
hne a musí vlézt do nejbližšího
vagonu. A tak to jde
až do Wídně, kde
někteří ovablici vorou

15

A few days later they woke us up early in the morning and we went down to the railway station. At first we thought we would travel by truck. There were about thirty of them lined up in the open area, all Studebakers, of course. And so we took leave of this camp and continued on, with all sorts of thoughts.

JOURNEY BY TRAIN

Here we were, once again, at a railway station, but this time, as we boarded the train, we got into passenger coaches, not freight cars. Although we were pretty crowded, we could still sit down. There were Russians everywhere, men and women. Next to us was a pile of luggage, and on it sat a boorish young Russian whose hands were permanently under the skirts of his partner, a healthy, cheerful Russian woman.

Two hours later we left the station. We moved slowly, very slowly, but at least we were in motion. Everywhere there were badly damaged rails and primitively repaired bridges, and we moved forward cautiously. We passed ruined towns, broken bridges, derailed trains, and cars and locomotives that had been shot up. Then somebody came and announced that when the train stopped, one person from each group should go ahead and fetch bread and margarine from the first freight car. Three of our boys got out at the next stop and rushed forward, but there was already a long lineup. Before their turn came, the train began moving again and they had to climb aboard the nearest carriage. And thus it went on until we reached Vienna, where some brave individuals left the train and went into the nearby gardens to gather fruit.

Everywhere there were ruins and more ruins. In Vienna we shunted back and forth for a long time, but at last we got back on track and that night, we stopped in Wiener Neustadt.[41] Here we got out, along with about twenty brave souls who were heading to Bohemia and Moravia. The others traveled on, but we were soon reunited.

Meanwhile we lay down on benches, or tables, or on whatever was available. I climbed onto a cupboard in an empty station cafeteria. At about midnight, they led us away to a destroyed station building, where we slept on the floor till morning.

WIENER NEUSTADT

Near the station there was a pump where we washed a bit and then walked in the park and the area around the railway station. From a nearby window we heard a radio, then we heard people speaking in Czech. The majority of the buildings here were damaged, but the railway station was the worst.

One of the adults in our group went to ask where we should go, and around noon we set off again, through the town to another suburb, where there were several wooden barracks and refugees everywhere, mainly from the Czechoslovak Republic. We had to be disinfected again and, with a confirmation in hand that this had been done; we were issued a permit to leave for home. We had to fill out many forms for the Russian authorities.

With this slip of paper, we walked a good distance to a former factory where we were given accommodation. We found bunks and made ourselves comfortable. We received bread and tobacco. We examined the ruined tracks and often went into the local cemetery where there were many interesting things to see. The entire history of the town was right there, on gravestones. The war (air raids) had been responsible for many civilian graves; then there were graves of German soldiers, and finally red burial mounds of Red Army soldiers. We were also present at the funeral of a female Russian officer. It was very moving and beautiful—with weeping Russian women soldiers, salvos, and singing.

Some Czech soldiers were stationed in that factory and they later went home with us. There were also several vehicles belonging to the Czechoslovak army. We were given soup in the Russian field kitchen.

We stayed in Wiener Neustadt for about a week, maybe less, I do not recall exactly.

Then we got news that the track to Bratislava was completely ruined and we would have to go *per pedes* [Latin for "on foot"] for about one hundred kilometers. It was estimated that it would take three days. Everyone who had some luggage packed it up. (I had only my toilet kit, a mug, a loaf of bread, and a box of tobacco that I intended to trade for something else.) Someone found a small cart, and there were

z vlaku do okolních zahrad na oře.
Všude jen trosky a zas trosky. Ve Vídni
jsme dlouho šiborali, ale přec jsme se
konečně vymotali a v noci jsme zastavli
ve Wiener Neustadt.

Zde jsme vystoupili ještě asi s 20ti
odvážlivci, kteří jeli do Čech a na Moravu.
Ostatní jeli dál, ale shledali jsme se
s nimi brzy.

My jsme ztrnu ulehli na syrý
lavici, stoli a vůbec vše se dalo. Já
si neobsolad klesl na skříň v vračdním
bufetu. Až o půlnoci nás dodali na
rozbořenou nádražní budovu, kde jsme
useni spali až do rána.

Tábor ve V. N. M.

Blízko nádraží byla pumpa, tam jsme se

místa v podobě náhrobků. Válka připravila
mnoho hrobů civilistům (nálety) pak hroby německých
vojínů a na konec červené mohyly krasnoarmějců.
Byli jsme také přítomni pohřbu jedné ruské důstojnice.
Bylo to velmi dojemné a krásné. Plačící ruské
vojačky, salvy, atd.

V té kovárně měli stanici také četu vojáků, kteří
pak s námi jeli domů. Polévku jsme dostávali v
posádkové ruské kuchyni. Bylo zde také několik
aut Československé armády.

Ve vídeňském novém místě jsme byli asi týden,
snad méně, nevím již přesně.

Pak přišly zprávy zprávy o tom, že trať do Bratislavy
je úplně rozbitá a že půjdeme pěšky až 100 km.
Rozvrhnuto na 3 dny. Každý, kdo měl nějaké
zavazadlo (já měl mycí potřeb, hrnek, bochník chleba

18

Pěšky do VLASTI.

Dlouhý had se ohnul po cestách a táhl k Bratislavě. První odpočinek byl až v Eisenstadtě, kde jsme jedli rýži a jablka v okolních zahradách.

Vlekli jsme se pomalu hrozným vedrem po rozpálených cestách. Odpočívali jsme kde se dalo, pili vodu, jedli meruňky, kterých bylo na cestách mnoho, trhali třešně a žebrovali chléb ze vlastní zásoby. První noc jsme spali v příkopě. Nikde jsem nesehnal deku, tak se mi nespalo ani tak špatně. Ráno se šlo dál, stále vpřed. Ztratili jsme se hlavního voje. Nezbývalo nás už mnoho. Největší polovička zůstala za námi. Druhou noc jsme se uchýlili v nějaké stodole, ale vyhnali nás, a tak jsme spali zase venku

20

two or three hay wagons pulled by horses, which some enterprising Carpathian Ukrainian Jews had stolen. Also Skoba found something that had wheels, and he and Werner tied their luggage to it. It later fell apart.[42]

And finally, one morning, we set off. The large procession wound through the town. At the head of it was a car with a Russian officer and a Slovak sergeant full of luggage belonging to those thieves (*Ganevs*). Gradually, the procession stretched out over many kilometers as those who could not keep up fell behind. Some did not reach Bratislava until a week later. It was a motley procession. Again, we walked through the whole city, and set off in a northeasterly direction.

ON FOOT TO OUR HOMELAND

Our long snake wound its way towards Bratislava. The first rest stop was in Eisenstadt, where we ate red currants and apples from the surrounding gardens.

We trudged slowly along scorched roads in a terrible heat. We rested where we could, drank water, ate mulberries, which were plentiful along the road, and picked cherries, which we ate along with the bread we had with us. The first night we slept in a ditch. Somewhere I got hold of a blanket and slept quite well. In the morning we continued on, always moving forward. We managed to stay in the vanguard. There were not many of us; at least half our group lagged behind. The second night we settled down to pass the night in a barn but were driven out and had to sleep outdoors near the road. We were very tired. By the third day, the walking was very hard. But in the evening we saw Bratislava castle in the distance. It started to rain.

That night we slept on straw in a large farm. On the morning of the fourth day we set out early and soon overtook almost everybody else. We had to take detours because the bridges of the main roads were all in ruins. We came across thousands of horses that the Russians had stolen in Slovakia and driven away, along with cattle and carts.

At noon we pulled a few potatoes out of the field and boiled them. We encountered many Russians from various camps walking in the opposite direction. They were awful guys, drunk and the terror of the countryside. They plundered, stole, and killed. They carried beer, alarm clocks, women, and food. They rode on stolen horses and carts—a terrible rabble, the worst kind of riffraff—Russians and Ukrainians—a mob!

We hurried on and saw only plundered villages, the inhabitants hiding in the woods or locked up, beaten up and frightened. Eastern culture had paid them a visit. Who can blame these old, hard-working people in wartime? What were they guilty of? They lived without food in an area that was twice overrun by the war. Without crops, hungry, working hard. And now thugs like this had come along and taken everything they had left away from them, leaving their wives and daughters despoiled.

Petržalka:—Czechoslovak border guards checked our luggage and a short while later we crossed a pontoon bridge over the Danube. We were in the Republic.

Home Again

BRATISLAVA

We dragged ourselves along with our last strength. It was evening as we walked through the streets of Bratislava. People stopped, and turned around to stare at us. We looked terrible. They led us to a newly constructed building that was meant to be a department store. It now housed many refugees, who slept on the floor. We settled down in a small room on the fourth floor. In the evening we were given a piece of bread and coffee and a gentleman in the street, gave us twenty crowns. Soon after that we retired and immediately fell asleep after the grueling journey. At that time we had not yet completely recovered, and the strenuous trek had exhausted us.

We stayed in Bratislava for several days. After a long wait at the Jewish community center, we were given four hundred crowns. We ate

vypracovani kmeti na raice, roč byli vini. Bez jidla
žili v kraji kudy se 2x přehnula vojna. Bez viny
o hladu v těžké práci. A ted "přijdou takoví
lumpové", berou jim to posledni a požijou jim réz
a dcery.

　　Petržalka – prohlídka zavazadel céčkami
finouci a na chvili kráčíme přes pontonový most vo
Dunaj, jsme v Republice.

───────────

3. část

DOMA,
VE VLASTI

Bratislava – Praha – Kamenice –
– Štiřín – Skalice Č. – Náchod.
(Stručně.)

23

in the kitchen for the poor. The food was nothing special but it was better than what they gave to those who were being repatriated. For the first time, we even went to see a movie, "Ivan the Terrible."

Every day we waited at the repatriation office until our turn came. They issued us identification cards, sent us to a bath, gave us five hundred crowns, and the next day, we were off to Prague. A woman gave us a loaf of bread for the trip. We took a streetcar to the railway station and, without tickets, boarded an express train.

Our group gradually dispersed. Herz and Goldberger got out at Brno, where the train emptied out and we could sit in seats instead of standing in the corridor.[43] A man joined us and gave us sweet buns, a rare delicacy for us. Pavel Werner got off the train in Pardubice, and at two o'clock in the morning, when we arrived at Wilson station in Prague, there were only three of us left: Fink, Skoba and I.[44]

PRAGUE

The first thing we did was look for the repatriation office. It was closed and didn't open until 8:00 in the morning. We went to the Masaryk train station and slept the night under a counter.

In the morning, Harry left us and we went to the repatriation office, which was in Hybernská Street. There I met Mr. Berger, an acquaintance from Terezín. We were sent to a hostel on Petrské Square. Some people gave us money and a woman bought us a roll. We looked awful and everyone noticed us immediately.

At the Petrské hostel, I asked about relatives but they knew nothing. I still hoped my mother was alive, but I was beginning to have my doubts. The uncertainty was terrible.

They sent us to the Milič House where we were cordially received and told we had to be examined for lice and that after that, we would go to a convalescent center.[45] And so we went to Vinohrady. Some nits were found on me and I had to be deloused, and we were all brought back only late at night. In the morning, I went to Milič House again and was immediately driven to a convalescent home with the director, Mr. Pitter.

THE CONVALESCENT HOME

The car stopped in Olešovice, where some provisions were unloaded. We got out there as well and walked through a beautiful countryside to Kamenice. It was June twenty-ninth. The day before, in Prague, at the delousing station, had been my fifteenth birthday. But now I felt well. I walked with Skoba and a lady teacher to a pretty chateau named Štiřín, located in a large garden.

Here, for the first time, I ate again at a table with cutlery, slept in a bed, went on excursions and enjoyed freedom.

I started to correspond with the Horáčeks, the Bayerles, Rudolf Beck and with Věra, who told me the sad news about my mother's fate.[46] Later we went over to Štiřín.

Family Before the War

Michael Kraus
(b. 1930), ca. 1938

Some childhood friends in Náchod, May 31, 1934. From left: **Tomáš Beck**,
b. 1932, perished in Auschwitz II, son of Rudolf and Vilma Beck from
Náchod; they survived the camp. **Michael Kraus**. **Max Goldschmid**,
b. 1932, Michael's maternal cousin; he survived the Second World War
with his parents in Palestine. **Ivan Polák**.

Dr. Karel Kraus
(b. 1891; d. 1944),
1930s

Lotte Krausová (b. 1898; d. 1945) with her son
Michael, ca. 1935

The Terezín Newspaper "Kamarád"

During his time at Terezín, Michael Kraus wrote for "Kamarád," a newspaper published by boys in the Q 609 block. "Kamarád" contained comics, stories, and practical advice and served as a chronicle of life in the block. Its publication is a testament to the creativity and ingenuity of the boys who served on its editorial team.

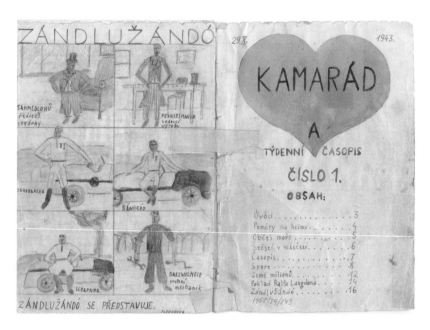

Title page of the newspaper "Kamarád," issue no. 1, November 29, 1943 (author: Ivan Polák).

Ivan Polák (b. 1929) shown here ca. 1934. Publisher and editor of the journal "Kamarád" from 1943–1944 in children's home Q 609 at Terezín. Deported to Terezín and Auschwitz II, died in the Dachau concentration camp on January 19, 1945.

LEV A MYŠKA.

Michal Kraus.

Michael Kraus, "In my Most Difficult Moment—Conversation with Mother"

Michael Kraus, "The Lion and the Mouse"

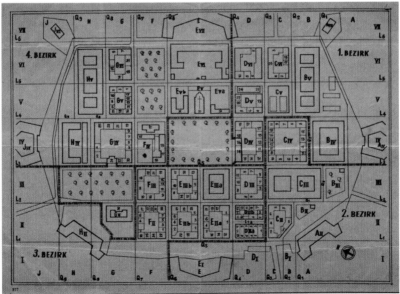

Plan of the Terezín Ghetto

The Other Deported Children

When the SS liquidated the so-called family camp (B.II.b) in early July 1944 in Auschwitz II (Birkenau), they chose eighty-nine boys between the ages of thirteen and fifteen to serve as workers and messengers. Some of them lived together with Michael Kraus in Gunskirchen (Austria) at the end of the war on May 5, 1945.

Jehuda (Jiří) Bakon (Yehuda Bacon, b. 1929), 1945. A major Israeli painter after the war, he had a 2011 exhibition in Prague.

Harry Fink (b. 1931), before the war

Harry Goldberger (b. 1931), after the war

Frank (Míša) Grünwald (b. 1932), 1945

Harry Osers
(b. 1929), 1954

Robert (Robin) Herz (b. 1930) and his brother
Martin (b. 1929, liberated in Auschwitz), 1945

Bedřich Steiner
(b. 1931), 1939

Jan Strebinger
(b. 1931), before
the war

Pavel Werner
(b. 1932), 1942

Transition to "Normal" Life

Věra Löwenbachová (later Feldmanová) and Rudolf and Vilma Beck were very important people in the life of Michael Kraus after his liberation from the concentration camp. These three allowed him to return to a "normal" life and were among the few who understood him at that time. Like Michael, they also lost their families in Auschwitz—Věra her husband and two small children, the Becks their little son Tomáš. Věra Feldmanová was an emotional and moral support for Michael; with her he found refuge from those who did not understand survivors. Until her death at age ninety, she was for him a bridge from the horrors of the Holocaust to a normal life.

Michael Kraus, 1945

Michael Kraus in a school group in Trčov, 1946

Věra Löwenbachová, b. Bondyová, after the war Feldmanová (b. 1910; d. 2001)

Vilma Becková (b. 1908; d. 1982),
end of the 1940s

Rudolf (Ruda) Beck (b. 1900; d.
1988) in Náchod, end of the 1940s

Some of the "Birkenau Boys" in 1994, in front of Block L 417 in Terezín. *Standing from left, back row*: Michael Kraus, Harry Osers, Walter Hacker (Austrian), Jiří Diamant. *Middle row*: Hanuš Fürnberg, Ota Fürth, Pavel Krajský, Ernst Hacker (Austrian), Harry Goldberger. *Front row*: Toman Brod, John Freund, Helmut Szprycer (Berlin), Jindřich Silberstein, Pavel Bergman. *Sitting*: Jehuda (Jiří) Bakon (Yehuda Bacon), Michael Honigwachs (Honey).

NOTES

1 SS is an abbreviation for *Schutzstaffel*, the armed organization of the NSDAP (Nazi party), created in 1925 and composed of fanatically loyal supporters of Adolf Hitler, who initially served as his bodyguard. At the peak of its power, the SS was led by Heinrich Himmler, who held the rank of *Reichsführer-SS*. In time, the SS came to dominate the governmental and security agencies in the Third Reich, including its extermination policies. As its logo, it used the Old German signs for "S," resembling two bolts of lightning on a black background.

2 All designations such as E I, B II, and E IV refer to buildings in the Terezín ghetto.

3 Jiří Fränkl was born in Hradec Králové on April 26, 1921; he and his family were sent to the Terezín ghetto on Transport Ci on December 21, 1942. He was a youth leader in Q 609. From there, he went voluntarily with his family on Transport Ds, on December 18, 1942, to Auschwitz, where he worked as a teacher and youth leader in the children's block. In 1944, he was transported to a labor camp in Schwarzheide. His parents perished in the gas chamber. While on the death march to Lübeck in 1945, he was liberated by the Red Army. On returning to Czechoslovakia, he studied English in the Faculty of Arts at Charles University in Prague and, in 1960, became an assistant professor at the Economic University. He emigrated with his family to England in 1968, where he continued to teach. He wrote a book called *The Blazing Sky*. He died on June 1, 1994, in London.

4 Boys between the ages of twelve and fifteen from home Q 609 contributed articles to the magazine "Kamarád." Míša's friend from Náchod, Ivan Polák (b. 1929), was the editor-in-chief. He carefully transcribed all the contributions and illustrated them with his own drawings. There was always only one original, which was "published" on Friday when he read it out loud to the other boys. Between 1943 and 1944, twenty-two issues were created and are kept at the memorial of Beit Terezín in the Givat Chaim Ichud kibbutz, Israel. Ivan Polák was sent to Auschwitz on Transport Eq on October 12, 1944. He died on January 19, 1945, in Dachau. In 1997, Ruth Bondy published a book in Hebrew about "Kamarád" in Israel (the book is out of print; an English translation does not exist).

5 This figure was later verified against the teaching material published in *Dokumenty z archivu Památníku Terezín* (Documents from the Terezín Archives). In January 1943, five transports from Terezín were sent to Auschwitz. From a total of 7,001 persons, only 96 survived, i.e., 1.37 percent.

6 Most of the members of the SS who had run Terezín escaped justice. Only a few were caught and tried before the Extraordinary People's Court in Litoměřice or tried in courts abroad. The commander of the camp, Siegfried Seidl, was captured in Austria and sentenced to death. His successor, Anton Burger, however, managed to escape twice and died in his nineties, never having been punished. The third and final commander of the camp,

Karl Rahm, was condemned to death by the Litoměřice court. Most of their fellow officers, however, were tried in absentia or never appeared in any court. For the most part, justice was never done.

7 Janeček used a Germanized version of his name, Janetschek. Although he commanded a unit of the Czech Protectorate constabulary (about 150 men) in the Terezín ghetto, most of whom were sympathetic to the prisoners, he was notorious for being as brutal as members of the SS.

8 According to various estimates, between 1.2 and 1.6 million people perished in Auschwitz. It was an extensive complex, divided into three major sectors. Auschwitz I was the main camp where mainly political enemies of the Reich were imprisoned. Auschwitz II-Birkenau was the largest in size and was intended as an extermination camp mainly for Jews. It was about three kilometers away from Auschwitz I. Auschwitz III-Monowitz was a camp for slave laborers who worked in the I. G. Farben Bunawerke, a chemical factory. It was about seven kilometers away from Auschwitz I.

9 B.II.b was the name given to a section of Auschwitz II-Birkenau where 2,504 people were forcibly brought from the Terezín ghetto by Transport Dr on December 15, 1943. Only 279 of those survived. Another transport (Ds) carrying 2,503 people was sent there on December 18. Of those, only 449 survived. Together with prisoners from Transports Dl and Dm in September, these people formed the so-called family camp (*Familienlager*).

10 Fritz Buntrock was commander of the family camp in Auschwitz II-Birkenau made up of Jewish prisoners from Terezín. He was sentenced to death in Krakow in 1947.

11 In addition to the family camp B.II.b, there was another family camp for Gypsies, B.II.e.

12 March 7, 1944, was the birthday of Tomáš Garrigue Masaryk, the founding president of Czechoslovakia. On that day, the September transport was transferred to the adjacent camp B.II.a. All 3,793 persons were killed in the gas chambers during the early hours of March 9. It was the largest mass slaughter of (Czechoslovak) citizens committed by the Germans during the six-year occupation.

13 These were Transports Dz, Ea, and Eb, sent from Terezín on the 15th, 16th, and 18th of May 1944, with 7,503 people. Of these, only 401 survived and were liberated.

14 Blechhammer was one of the auxiliary camps of Auschwitz, where prisoners worked in chemical factories. Bergen-Belsen was a prisoner-of-war camp in Germany from 1940 on, and a concentration camp after 1942. In 1945, prisoners from various concentration camps in the East were taken there. Buchenwald, a concentration camp in central Germany near Weimar, had already been set up in 1937. The Americans liberated the camp on April 11, 1945.

15 Stutthof (Sztutowo in Polish) was an extensive Nazi German concentration camp in a wooded region near the Baltic port city of Gdańsk. It was founded in September 1939.

16 The *Sonderkommando* was a special group of prisoners (about 800 men, at first exclusively

Jews, but later Russians and Poles as well) whose job it was to gas the prisoners, clear the gas chambers afterward, burn the bodies in the crematoria of Auschwitz II, extract gold teeth from the victims, and other tasks. Members of the *Sonderkommando* were separated from the rest of the prisoners. They lived in the men's camp B.II.d in Block 11. Finally, they were housed right in the attics above the crematoria. There was no escaping from the *Sonderkommando*, only death.

17 Neu Berun, Bierun in Polish, was a community in Upper Silesia near Auschwitz.

18 In the autumn of 1944, a total of eleven transports went from Terezín to Auschwitz: from Ek on September 28 to Ev on October 28, the transports included a total of 18,402 persons, of whom 1,574 survived.

19 Rudolf Beck (b. 1900 in Vrchlabí; d. 1988 in Náchod) wrote a memoir called *Recollections for My Daughter*, about his imprisonment in Terezín and Auschwitz; his daughter, Maria Talafantová, published it in Náchod in 1995. Tomáš Löwenbach (b. 1926), from Hronov, survived imprisonment in Terezín, Auschwitz, and Mauthausen. His story is recorded in the book *Room 127, The House of Youth Q708, Terezín*, published in Plzeň in 2007.

20 Loslau is a community in the south of Poland; today, it is called Wodzislaw Slaski, about twenty kilometers northeast of Ostrava. It is about ninety kilometers from Auschwitz.

21 Mauthausen was a concentration camp in Austria that was among the very worst of the Nazi death camps. It was situated about thirty kilometers east of Linz, next to the small town of Mauthausen, close to the quarries. Through its gates passed about 335,000 prisoners from more than thirty countries, and more than 122,000 of those were killed; 4,500 were tortured to death in 1945 alone.

22 Míša Grünwald (original name František Michael Grünwald, b. August 30, 1932) went on Transport AAq from Prague to Terezín on July 13, 1942. From there, he was on Transport Dr to Auschwitz-Birkenau on December 15, 1943. In January 1945, he was on the death march from Auschwitz to Loslau. He was imprisoned in Mauthausen and Melk, liberated in Gunskirchen May 5, 1945, and lives in Indianapolis, Indiana (United States).

23 In German, the cloth was called *Drell*—a thinly woven fabric from which the prison uniforms were made.

24 Melk is an Austrian town on the Danube, whose dominating feature is a Baroque Benedictine monastery from the twelfth century.

25 Harry Osers (b. 1929) went on Transport Cc from Prague to Terezin on November 11, 1942. From there he went on Transport Dr to Auschwitz on December 15, 1943. In January 1945, he was on the death march from Auschwitz to Loslau. He was imprisoned in Mauthausen and Melk and liberated in Gunskirchen on May 5, 1945. He lived and died in Caracas, Venezuela.

26 Harry Goldberger (b. 1931) was on Transport Bi from Ostrava to Terezín on August 22, 1942. Then he was on Transport Dr to Auschwitz on December 15, 1943. In January 1945, he was

on the death march from Auschwitz to Loslau. He was imprisoned in Mauthausen and Melk, liberated in Gunskirchen May 5, 1945, and died in the United States in 1997.

27 Anti-aircraft cannons.

28 A reference to members of the SS.

29 Gunskirchen is a municipality in Austria; it was also a concentration camp.

30 Franta was the head room captain (*Stubendienst*) in the second camp in Mauthausen in 1945. No other information about him is known.

31 Wels is a city of about 60,000 in Austria, on the river Traun, twenty-seven kilometers west of Linz.

32 *Schutzpolizei* (or *Schupo*), from the German *schutz*, meaning "protective," refers to a division of the German police force whose main purpose was maintaining public order. In this case, they served as prison guards.

33 Harry Kraus [Karni] (b. 1931) was on Transport Ca from Prague to Terezín on October 24, 1942, and Transport Dr to Auschwitz on December 15, 1943. He was on the death march from Auschwitz to Loslau, imprisoned in Mauthausen and Melk, and liberated in Gunskirchen May 5, 1945. He lived and died in Tel Aviv.

34 It seems that the American army liberated the camp on May 4 and that we left the camp the following morning, on May 5, 1945. The author uses May 5, 1945, as the day of liberation. However, when he wrote his diary in Náchod, he erroneously used May 7 as the first day of freedom.

35 Harry Fink (b. 1931) was on Transport AAw from Prague to Terezín on August 3, 1942, and Transport Ds to Auschwitz on December 18, 1943. He was liberated in Gunskirchen on May 5, 1945. He lived in Karlové Vary and died there in 2006 after a long illness.

36 Germany surrendered May 8, 1945.

37 Some of the survivors have different recollections of this incident.

38 David L. Filtzer, MD, was a US Army doctor who cared for Míša in Hörsching. Later, he sent care packages and letters to Míša in Náchod. When they finally met again in Cambridge, Massachusetts (1980), Dr. Filtzer was a prominent surgeon in Baltimore. Unfortunately, in 1988 he died of cancer at a relatively young age.

39 Gorila was and still is the nickname of (Honza) Jan Strebinger (b. 1931), who was on Transport M from Prague to Terezín on December 14, 1941, and Transport Eb to Auschwitz on May 18, 1944. In January 1945, he was on the death march to Loslau. Imprisoned in Mauthausen and Melk, he was liberated in Gunskirchen on May 5, 1945. He lives in São Paulo, Brazil. Míša does not know how he got his nickname; everyone still calls him Gorila today, including his family and children.

40 The Studebakers were trucks that the Americans provided to the Soviet army.

41 Wiener Neustadt is a town in Austria about fifty kilometers south of Vienna.

42 Skoba was the nickname for Bedřich Steiner (b. 1931), who was on Transport Cv from Prague to Terezín on March 6, 1943, and Transport Dr to Auschwitz on December 15, 1943. In January 1945, he was on the death march to Loslau. Imprisoned in Mauthausen and Melk, he was liberated in Gunskirchen on May 5, 1945. He lives in Mexico. Pavel Werner (b. 1932) was on Transport Cg from Pardubice to Terezín on December 9, 1942, and Transport Dz to Auschwitz on May 15, 1944. In January 1945, he was on the death march to Loslau. Imprisoned in Mauthausen and Melk, he was liberated in Gunskirchen May 5, 1945. He lives in Prague, where he is active as treasurer of *Terezínská Iniciativa*. He gives talks in schools and teacher training courses about his childhood experiences in Nazi concentration camps.

43 Robin Herz (b. Robert in 1930) was taken by Transport Ae from Brno to Terezín on March 29, 1942, and by Transport Eb to Auschwitz May 18, 1944. In January 1945, he was on the death march from Auschwitz to Loslau. Imprisoned in Mauthausen and Melk, he was liberated in Gunskirchen on May 5, 1945. After the war he lived in Toronto, Canada, where he died in 2000.

44 Wilson Station is Prague's main railway station.

45 Milíč House (*Milíčův dům*)—which today is a nursery school of the same name—was founded and given this name by the Christian humanist Přemysl Pitter (b. Prague 1895; d. Zurich 1976). The house was opened in the Prague quarter of Žižkov on Christmas Day 1933. It was meant to educate the poorest children in Žižkov, who came to it for schooling. After 1937, at least 150 children were sheltered there, including the children of parents who had to flee Nazi Germany. During the Second World War, Pitter mainly helped Jews, and after liberation he requisitioned the confiscated chateaux of Štiřín, Olešovice, Kamenice, and Lojovice, where, with his collaborators, he looked after forsaken Jewish orphans who had gone through the concentration camps. From May 1945 to May 1947, 810 orphans were cared for in these chateaux. Later, he sheltered German children of families who had been deported from Czechoslovakia after the war. After the communist *coup d'état* in 1948, Pitter had to flee, because he had openly criticized the way the Germans were treated during the expulsions. He lived in Germany, and later in Switzerland, where he continued to help people and publicize their plight. His faithful assistant from the 1920s on was Olga Fierzová (b. Baden 1900; d. Affoltern am Albis in Switzerland 1990). Both Pitter and Fierzová were later honored by Yad Vashem with the title "Righteous Among the Nations," given to those who saved Jews.

46 The Horáčeks include Líza Horáčková, a cousin; her mother, Marie Steinerová, was the sister of Lotte Krausová, Míša's mother. The Bayerles include Dr. Václav Bayerle and Valerie, née Strassová, from Náchod. Rudolf Beck, from Náchod, and his wife Vilma survived the Holocaust. After the war, they provided Míša with a sensitive place of refuge. Vera is Věra Löwenbachová, née Bondyová, from Česká Skalice. After the war, she became Feldmanová. Her story was recorded in Věra Vlčková's book, *As Long as I Breathe, I Hope*, published in Náchod in 2006.